ST PETROCK'S CHURCH

PARRACOMBE

Published by
Parracombe Archaeology & History Society

ISBN: 978-1-8384822-3-7

Compiled by Karen Farrington

With special thanks to: Torrington Cavaliers and the people of Parracombe for financial support, and all those who contributed.

Contents

Preface

So many churches in this country suffered at the hand of Victorians and their 'restorations' which, although largely carried out with good intentions, often swept away centuries of historic development, resulting in many churches feeling sanitised, lacking in character and, in some cases, being lost completely.

Fortunately for us, a few strong-willed individuals recognised the harm being caused, and acted. William Morris, who was at the forefront of the movement against the restorations, founded the Society for the Protection of Ancient Buildings (SPAB) in 1877, as a way of highlighting this issue. SPAB is today the longest-established building conservation body in the UK and its ideas and themes constitute the mainstream thinking of building conservation around the world.

At the heart of the 'SPAB Manifesto' is the idea that the protection of building fabric should be the priority, and that careful and considered repair is in the best interests of the building, as opposed to restoration or attempting to turn the clock back to what is believed to be a previous ideal. Fundamentally the SPAB way of thinking came from the mind of John Ruskin who, in his 'Seven Lamps of Architecture', described restoration as 'a lie from beginning to end'. As you will see in this fascinating book, the fact that St Petrock's Church is still here today is due in no small part to Ruskin himself.

Whenever I am passing by Parracombe with visitors to Exmoor I make special effort to stop and show them this remarkable building, to demonstrate that not all churches conform to the Victorian ideals we now consider to be the norm. Its monuments, the painted texts, the wonderful box pews and the fascinating graffiti, which is still coming to light, tell us so much about past generations that have used this space.

The site has likely drawn pilgrims since the 6th century, a time when the Roman occupation of Britain was still a relatively recent memory. The existing building is clearly much later, with the earlier sections likely to date from the 1100s, and whenever I am in buildings of this age, it is impossible not to think of the thousands of social events that must have taken place in and around its walls.

As this book so wonderfully demonstrates, one of the chief joys of the building lies in its graveyard which has a marvellous array of chest tombs and gravestones, some of which are listed structures in their own right. These can give intriguing insights to the lives of those who lived and died in Parracombe. It is impossible not to notice how few of those buried here reached old age. As is common, there are numerous unmarked graves of the poor and, given the age of the site, there could well be thousands of burials.

The building has been at the heart of the community of Parracombe for centuries. It has witnessed wars, revolts, plagues, celebrations and unimageable technical advances. Given the fondness that the community of Parracombe has for the building, I have no doubt many more generations will be able to enjoy it. Of which I am sure Ruskin would be proud.

Thomas Thurlow, Historic Buildings Officer, Exmoor National Park Authority

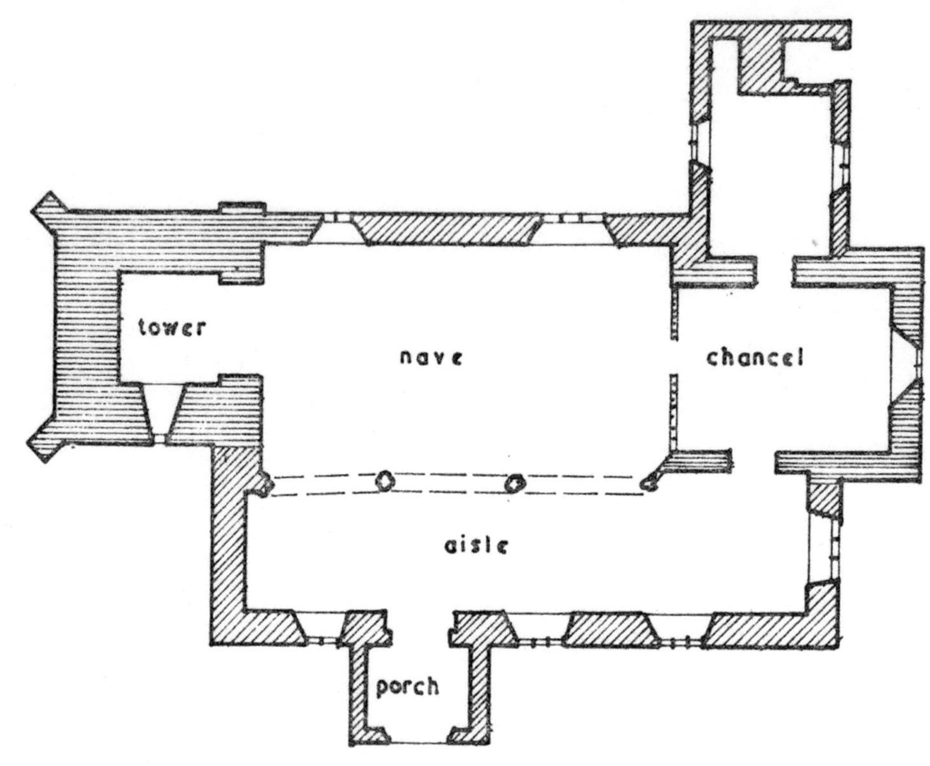

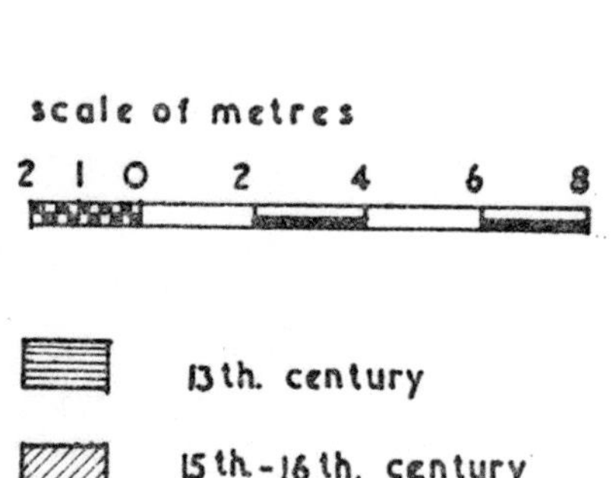

St Petrock's, Parracombe plan of the church from the Churches Conservation Trust's guide leaflet (taken from the original edition: Bulmer-Thomas n.d., but c.1970).

St Petrock's Church, Parracombe

'[St Petrock's] has escaped the ravages of the modern restorers....consequently it retains many points of interest, such as the screen with its post-reformation tympanum, the three decker, the mixture of old oak benches and high pews, the seats for the choir and band rising one above the other at the west end. It is of all ages – the tower, Transition Norman; the church, Early English, Perpendicular and 17th century. It was restored to the extent of being made wind and weather-tight but without interfering with any of its internal fittings.'

Rev JF Chanter 1917

Who was St Petrock?

St Petrock was described as handsome, courteous, charitable and wise.

Probably born in South Wales, Petrock – Petroc, Petrocus or Pedrog – lived in the sixth century, and was famous for sheltering a hunted stag.

He is most closely associated with Cornwall, where Padstow and Bodmin became centres of worship dedicated to him. However, there are 17 churches in Devon, one in Somerset, at least three in Wales, seven in Cornwall and more than 30 in Brittany, France, that bear his name.

Petrock is believed to have studied theology in Ireland and later made pilgrimages to Rome and Jerusalem, so he was surprisingly well-travelled for a man of the era.

One of the few accounts of his life, uncovered during the 20th century at the Ducal Library in Gotha, Germany, relates numerous miracles he carried out and describes him as handsome, courteous, prudent, modest, humble, a cheerful giver, charitable and wise. One must accept this glowing eulogy was made through the prism of devout faith. Soon after his death in Bodmin, on 4 June 564, it is believed a humble church was raised in Parracombe, replaced some five centuries later by a stone building.

In the same era, a disgruntled canon stole Petrock's bones from Bodmin and carried them off to the Abbey of St Meen in Brittany, France. The ivory casket was eventually returned via the court of Henry II at Winchester, where the King is said to have given a silk pall to cover the sacred relic. In parallel, there's an enduring story that the same king ordered the killers of Thomas Becket at Canterbury, in 1170, to build or renovate the church tower at Parracombe as part of their penance. It's an intriguing but unproven tale.

Keeping up appearances

Humble as it now may seem, St Petrock's Church was once the pivot around which village life played out. It was likely the 'original core' of the village, according to Hazel Riley and Rob Wilson-North in their book, '*A Field Archaeology of Exmoor*'.

The first known rector was Stephen St Aubyn, in 1284. Medieval squires of Parracombe, the St Aubyn family moved to Alfoxton in the Quantocks in the 15th century, although they maintained enduring links with the village. The family name crops up throughout church history, with numerous descendants acting as rectors or church patrons. None are apparently buried in the graveyard.

What else was in and around the village at the time? Centuries before the stone church was built, the nearby terrain had been re-modelled when a Bronze Age cemetery crept across Exmoor's skyline. Chapman Barrows, above the church, comprises about a dozen mounds, deemed to be burial chambers and long since emptied of any goods. In the same vicinity, there is a mortuary enclosure where dead bodies were once left to be stripped by scavengers: a group of diminutive standing stones known as the quincunx and, more impressive still, a single, prominent one. This slim menhir, the tallest prehistoric monument on Exmoor, is made from slate and known as the Longstone. According to a report by the village history group: 'The landscape around the Longstone contains extensive archaeological remains dating from the Neolithic period (5,000 years ago) until recent times.'

Below this ancient and distinctive silhouette, the village was dominated by a much later addition. The motte and bailey castle at its heart was built after the Norman invasion of 1066, a symbol of power and domination from these new overlords. In his guide to St Petrock's, church Ivor Bulmer-Thomas contends the castle is not ancient, rather the spoil from the construction of the Lynton and Barnstaple Railway. As the castle appears on maps drawn long before the building of the railway, we know that on this point, at least, he was wrong.

In low winter sunlight, remnants of ridge and furrow ploughing systems from the medieval period become apparent at various locations around the village. It's not entirely clear where these arable farmers lived as most dwellings have surely been covered by others or reclaimed by the land.

The earthy lines are among a very few clues about the rural life that unfolded in Parracombe, between the construction of Holwell Castle and the Victorian era. During centuries, hardy worshippers surely battled their way to the draughty hill-top church. Yet there is little to shed light on their lifestyle. It's hard to get a sense of pastoral life from dry records of long-forgotten leases and historic property ownership, or lists of tax payers and the like.

- Thanks to research by Audrey M Erskine, we know there were ten tax payers in Parracombe in 1332, with one of them being a woman, Isabel de Sancto Albyno.
- Seven archers were recorded in the 1569 Muster Roll, along with four pikemen, and one

harquebusier, a man who had one of the earliest guns that was fired while supported by wooden staff.

- In 1753, a questionnaire sent out via Exeter Cathedral noted that the number of baptisms and burials that typically took place each year amounted to six.
- From various reports down the centuries, we know the church has also been known both as St Helen's and St Peter's.

Whatever its name, the problems of keeping the old church in good order have always been in evidence.

At one stage, the vestry was used as a school, which presumably enhanced the footfall there. But with every passing decade it seems attendance became increasingly patchy.

According to one observer, part of the problem may have been the number of absentee rectors down the ages. Writing in the introduction of a Devon & Cornwall Record Society book published in 1917, Rev John Frederick Chanter outlined how many clergymen of the distant past were rooted elsewhere, in times when travel over Exmoor was arduous – and even dangerous. Curates, who tended to enjoy less authority than rectors, were left in charge.

Chanter was born in Barnstaple in 1853 and graduated from Jesus College, Cambridge, aged 26. In his early thirties he became rector of Parracombe and maintained a keen interest in village history.

In the book, Rev Chanter, a champion of St Petrock's, goes back to Richard Corne, who was the clergyman in charge there when national edicts governing the keeping of registers were drawn up by Henry VIII's advisor Thomas Cromwell. Thus it became Corne's task to take notes about who was baptised, married or buried by the church and keep them in a locked coffer, according to the law. Corne was, it seems, a pluralist, accommodating the detail of different Christian faiths at a time when religious tenets were a burning political issue. His 'broad church' approach served him well as he was in post from 1510 for more than 50 years. During this time, Henry VIII triggered the Reformation that severed the English church from Rome; his son and successor Edward ruled as an unyielding Protestant; Henry's daughter Mary then took the throne as a vengeful Catholic; only to be replaced by Elizabeth I in 1558, another Protestant. It must have been tricky political territory to negotiate for rural rectors like Corne, who died in 1561.

Afterwards there came a series of absent rectors. Corne's replacement John Heron was based in Alverdiscott while his successor, Conan Bryant, was also the rector of neighbouring Challacombe. Conan's son John then stepped in and split duties in Parracombe with those in the far-more-distant West Worlington. After him came John Hayne, distracted by his role as chaplain to the Earl of Bath.

Next in line was Edmund Fountayne, who clearly spent some time in the village as daughter Mary was baptised at St Petrock's on 23 January 1635. But after that the family went to live in Parkham. During his tenure, all men had to pledge loyalty to King Charles I and the Protestant faith as politicians sought to avert the growing religious divide in the country. In the 1641 Protestation Oath returns, the names of 76 men from Parracombe are recorded in the same handwriting. In addition, there are six signatures, belonging to Fountayne, churchwardens James Norman and Giles Ware, overseers Walter Lock and Simon Berrie and Constable Richard Blackemore [sic]. Of this list of names, none are to be found in today's graveyard.

Fountayne's son-in-law, John Newell, took over and has a memorial inside the church, although he lived – and died - in Combe Martin. We know a bit more about his life and times as his will was kept for posterity by the National Archives. Its contents are listed later in the book.

When John Blackmore became rector at Parracombe in 1681, he was the first senior resident clergyman for 200 years, according to Chanter.

A stand-out feature of St Petrock's is the boarded Georgian screen.

After Rev Blackmore's death in 1720, there were some more notable in-name-only rectors attached to Parracombe. During a 30 year tenure in the second half of the 18th century, Lancelot St Aubyn visited the village only once, on Sunday, 4 June 1769. A decade later, he admitted he had not been able to serve any church for several years and that a curate, paid £35 a year, lived at Parracombe's 'Parsonage House'.

St Aubyn's great nephew and successor, Lancelot Gravenor, didn't live in Parracombe either.

By the mid-19th century, Rev John Pyke was at the helm. He became rector of St Petrock's in 1826, a year after graduating from Oxford, and remained there for more than 40 years, until his death. Soon after he arrived in the village, he had his parsonage built, now known as Heddon Hall.

For centuries, there's scant evidence about the faithful congregation's experience as they endured services in all seasons, with box pews their best protection against the howling draught. However, Parracombe resident Arthur Smyth, an author and regular newspaper correspondent, bequeathed us a local history, written in about 1876, and his words offer some insight about what went on in Victorian times. It seems inclement weather might not have been the only reason for people deserting the pews.

At the time Smyth was writing, there was a vigorous rivalry between the established Church of England and the Methodist movement, spearheaded in the 18th century by Charles Wesley. National tensions were reflected in Parracombe – and, significantly, Smyth was the son of the local Wesleyan preacher.

Of Pyke, Smyth wrote: 'In his younger days [he] was of a hearty and genial disposition, and he at least fulfilled those of his clerical duties that the Church demanded if not the Biblical ones.'

But later support for the established church apparently dwindled, with Smyth observing: '[Pyke] kept aloof from his parishioners and never visited the sick except, at the last moment, to administer the

Sacrament to the dying.'

According to Smyth, Pyke's father was 'a tailor and draper' in Cross Street, Barnstaple, until, in 1807, he became a partner in a bank, where he made the family's fortune.

During Pyke's tenure in Parracombe, the population never fell below 400, living in about 75 households.

When his death came in 1868, it was sudden. Pyke apparently fell ill after being called to baptise a child at the far reaches of the parish, in poor weather. His replacement was Rev Louis Courtier Biggs, who tried to lure back the faithful by installing a large harmonium at a cost of 40 guineas. (According to village reporter Arthur Smyth: 'The chief player is Miss Helena Crocombe but the instrument is too hard for a lady to play.') At the same time, the Wesleyan Chapel at the heart of the village had got new seats, replacement windows and a fully functioning stove. Efforts by Rev Biggs to compete with the chapel in terms of heating turned into a risky business. One Sunday afternoon in 1869, in the depths of winter, the stove he had installed ignited, although thankfully the blaze was swiftly extinguished.

With his efforts frustrated, Rev Biggs was reduced to asking his congregation to sign an abiding agreement to worship only with the Church of England.

Unsurprisingly, that ruse didn't work either and our 19th century informant Smyth wrote: 'The parishioners did not like him calling on them unexpectedly in a friendly pastoral kind of way, they having been long accustomed to the previous rector's easy fulfillment of clerical duties. Perhaps they were afraid he would call when they were doing something wrong; at any rate they soon got tired of him.' (On the positive side, Smyth acknowledges him as a splendid musician who trained a capable choir of young voices.)

It seems villagers already ill-disposed towards Biggs were all too ready to listen to gossip that linked him romantically to the Exciseman's wife. They petitioned the patron of the church, Mr Pyke Nott, to get rid of him and Biggs left with a financial inducement in hand, going on to become a Christian missionary in Malaysia.

The next incumbent was Rev Peter Nettleton Leakey who, according to Smyth, became infamous in the village for his penny-pinching ways. It was during his watch that the church building was considered dangerously unstable and concern soon evolved into calls for a new one. But plans drawn up in the 1870s to build a church in the heart of the village weren't universally popular.

Once alerted by Leakey, art critic and polymath John Ruskin branded the proposed demolition 'an act of vandalism' and offered £10 towards the construction of a new church on the condition the existing one was left alone. More on his campaign later.

With agreement that the dark, damp interior of St Petrock's could act as a mortuary, the necessary £3,000 was soon raised for the building of Christ Church. Two bells were transferred from St Petrock's and the last service held in the old church was on 13 October 1878, just a week before the unfinished Christ Church opened its doors, although burials continued at the old church even after the new one was opened. According to the Church Register of the time: 'The [new] churchyard was also consecrated, but it is not to be used for burials (except under very special circumstances) while there is room for internments in the old churchyard.'

The old church always had its charms. St Petrock's is thought to have been the last church in Devon in which singing was supported by a band of musicians. But it was undeniably neglected. In his 'History of Parracombe', Arthur Smyth described it like this: 'The internal part of the tower, like the rest of the building, is very ruinous so as to be ascended with considerable danger …The church yard is small and well-filled tho' not very nicely kept up.'

When Christ Church was opened, a North Devon Journal report clearly indicates the villagers had surely fallen out of love with historic St Petrock's, even when other more eminent souls had not.

'The building of an entirely new church is an uncommon occurrence, for our ancestors in the long past who manifested the reality of their faith by rearing houses for the worship of God did their work so substantially that after the wear and tear of centuries the edifices as a rule need only to be 'restored' as the phrase goes, not rebuilt.'

But St Petrock's was an exception, the report insisted, as 'so dilapidated is its condition that to thoroughly repair it would be virtually to rebuild it and would involve as great an expense'. Moreover, it was, the report said, 'entirely destitute' of any features that warranted preservation!

'It is a very incarnation of architectural ugliness and that especially in recent years, since dilapidations have made it more unsightly still, the people of Parracombe could have worshipped in it with any degree of heartiness is a strong proof of the robustness of their piety.'

But finally neglect inspired a fresh affection for St Petrock's in a subsequent generation.

James Pyke, son of the former rector of Parracombe, left money in his will for its upkeep, with the interest from the bequest covered small-scale repairs. When costly maintenance to the roof was needed, the village formed a committee led by Reverend Chanter and sought subscriptions from residents.

To mark some major work being completed, Reverend Chanter held two services on one Sunday there, with the evening service attended by 143 people.

A local newspaper report said: 'For 14 years the only sound heard in the building has been that of the funeral service and it seemed weird and singular to find a large congregation taking fresh possession and waking up the echoes of the dead with the voice of song.'

Chanter began a tradition of using the church every other Sunday. But still the challenge of the church's upkeep remained and difficulties were exacerbated by thunderstorm damage in 1908.

The lightning strike in January that year was dramatically relayed in the local paper.

'At Parracombe never within the memory of any living person has a thunderstorm caused such serious

Graffiti was carved into pews shielded from the pulpit by stone pillars.

damage as the storm of yesterday. The old church of St Peter which stands on the hill about a quarter of a mile from the village and which has braved the storms of centuries has sustained almost irreparable damage.

'At about 11.30 there was an exceptionally vivid flash of lightning followed immediately by two distinct crashes of thunder which appeared to shake the earth.

'One of the pinnacle of a large portion of the corner of the tower were torn away and a large quantity of masonry fell from the southern side of the tower, leaving a hole several feet square . . . one large stone weighing at least three quarters of a hundredweight was hurled over 100 ft from the church . . . the pulpit is splintered. In the east end there are large fissures in the walls which appear to be twisted out of shape. Nearly all the glass in the windows has been smashed.'

A plaque on the church reveals what happened next.

Daisy wheels, like this, reflect a belief in good and evil spirits.

'This tower five Windows the east end porch roofs and pulpit were injured by lightning on 28 January 1908 and were restored the same year by public subscription and a lightning conductor and bell were provided and Martinhoe's disused font brought here.

John Frederick Chanter, rector
Robert St John Allison
John Creek, Churchwardens'

Still, the battle to keep the church building in good order continued, the costs falling to villagers who now had to help pay for the upkeep of two churches.

In the twenties, the tradition of having two services a year was established. Given the lack of heating, both tended to be in the summer and were often on successive summer Sundays around the August bank holiday, a day off particularly welcomed by agricultural labourers which was introduced in 1871. Initially, August bank holidays were at the beginning of the month until finally being knocked back by a few weeks to the month's end almost 100 years later.

When St Petrock's hosted the services, the collections were earmarked for the its repair fund. Record books reveal some of the figures being raised. In 1920, the sum was a mighty £8 16s 3d, the following year there were two services held on consecutive Sundays that yielded £7 13s 8d. But these were high markers in the decade. In 1922, the amount raised was £5 5s 2d. Two years later, the total was £6 7s 5d, although notes in the register imply 181 people attended two services there, held on August 5 and 12. The equivalent services in 1927, both held in July, raised just £3 12 3d.

Britain was in an economic slump, and St Petrock's wasn't the only good cause to which residents contributed. Typically, the Christmas Day collection went to the Waifs and Strays Society, now known as the Children's Society. St Dunstan's, the charity created to help blind veterans, was supported by the congregation as was the Mothers' Union. There were one-off collections too, like one taken in January 1928 for victims of the Westminster flood, when the Thames burst its banks, killing 14 people and rendering thousands more homeless. But the most regular collections were taken for the Diocesan Fund and used to maintain Christ Church.

Without cash, the church fabric continued to decline. A letter dated 2 December 1935 from Herbert Read, an Exeter-based sculptor and carver, expresses concern about the prized screen in St Petrock's. Read wrote: 'I find it is in a very bad state of repair and, unless it can be thoroughly restored, I would strongly recommend leaving it as it is'. Despite the earlier mishap he advised installing a stove, to be lit occasionally during wet weather to help keep the damp at bay. The decay of the screen, he thought, had been accelerated by moisture in the atmosphere.

During the Second World War, the services at St Petrock's continued on an annual basis but cash yielded to the collection plate was limited, amounting to just £6 12 3d in 1944.

On 2 August 1945, the North Devon Journal reported the two August services would continue, claiming: 'Visitors to North Devon will be as interested as residents in the arrangements whereby the historic 10th century Church of St Petrock's, which was founded, however, in the days of King Arthur of the Round Table, is to be used for all services on the first two Sundays of August'.

In 1951 the amount donated in six services held over two consecutive Sunday in August, was £5 14s 5d.

Carved pew ends, thought to date from medieval times and described in one 19th century book as 'worm-eaten oak', had long since been removed.

Once again, any repairs that took place were followed by slow deterioration. A letter, that appeared in the local newspaper in 1954 from a correspondent who signed himself FJS, lamented the condition in which he found St Petrock's.

'When I went to see the old church which I remembered so well I was very disappointed by an obvious lack of care and attention.

'The grass was almost as high as the gravestones and some of the older stones seem to have disappeared altogether.

'Inside the church itself the ivy was coming through from outside and in one place the ceiling had fallen down.

'When I saw on the parish balance sheet that a loan of £250 had been made to the new church . . . . I could not help feeling that some of this money could have been well used to give better care to the church which awakes many fond memories among the older generations and which itself is an historic monument of no mean value.'

Meanwhile, the financial burden on Parracombe's faithful continued to escalate. When Easter services were held at St Petrock's throughout the fifties, the sums raised were directed to rectory repairs. After the freezing temperatures recorded in the notorious winter of 1963, the boiler at Christ Church broke down and another fund was launched to replace it. A decade later, it was the clock at Christ Church that needed fixing. Set against this, books recording what was donated in services reveal a continuing slump. So there must have been a sense of relief when, on 25 June 1971, the church fell under the auspices of the newly created Redundant Churches Fund.

Today, St Petrock's is lodged firmly in the affections of visitors and villagers alike, but the problems of funding still loom large.

Now known as the Churches Conservation Trust, the charity in charge has spent a mighty £481,492 on conservation and maintenance at St Petrock's. Urgent repairs to the roof, nave and tower in 2002-3 amounted to £49,653 while in 2007 and 2008 a further £129,085 was needed. Another bill amounting to £83,449 was incurred after that.

St Petrock's, Parracombe

by Stuart R. Blaylock, B.A., Ph.D., F.S.A.

Dr Stuart Blaylock is a noted archaeologist and architectural historian whose researches cover ecclesiastical and domestic architecture from the medieval period to the 17th century and beyond. This section is based on notes for a lecture given by Dr Blaylock at the church on 20th September 2019. It was paired with a talk by Meriel O'Dowd of the CCT on the 19th century campaign to preserve the church entitled: 'Ruskin and the saving of St Petrock's church, Parracombe'. Because this aspect of the history of the church had been so well and so thoroughly covered by Meriel, in my talk I avoided any consideration of material related to this topic, and concentrated on what we can tell of the original medieval church; on its 18th century fittings and furnishings; and on what these tell us about church interiors of the time.

It is the preservation of this interior, in much the way it must have appeared to its 18th and early 19th century parishioners, that is the distinguishing glory of this church. This has, of course, been the subject of comment by many writers before; some of their enthusiasms appear in the quotations given hereafter:

'The church of St. Petrock, Parracombe has been placed on the statutory list of buildings of special architectural or historic interest in Grade A, and the accompanying description calls it 'the most interesting of all the churches in this part of Devon with a completely unspoiled Georgian interior'.'
(Bulmer-Thomas n.d., 1).

'The exceptional charm of the interior of the church is that it has never been restored. It is still much as it was two hundred years ago, a rare example of the usual furnishing of a modest village church, poor perhaps, but seemly.'
(Cherry and Pevsner 1989, 624).

'It is hard not to be bowled over by the charm of this church. Unlike its counterparts across Devon, this church was not improved by the Victorians. The consequence is a visit feels like stepping back in time to a country church two centuries ago.'
(Gray 2011, 132).

'The church was declared redundant on November 25th 1969 and was vested in Redundant Churches Fund on June 25th 1971, being the first church in the country recommended for vesting in the Fund by the Advisory Board for Redundant Churches. This is a measure of the importance with which the church is regarded nationally.'
(Bulmer-Thomas 1987, [6]).

'But fortunately this [total ruin] was averted by [the then rector's] successor, the Rev. Preb. J.F. Chanter, who took the old church in hand, effected necessary repairs, but made no alterations, so that we find here a little building still exhibiting all the early features of pre-reformation times, combined with the condition of the 17th and 18th centuries. [...] Nothing is straight in the building. No part of the church centres with any other part, neither the tower to the nave, nor the nave to the chancel, nor the screen to

either. The very flag stones of the floor dip irregularly, and the purlines of the cradle roof extend further on the north side of the chancel arch than on the south. The high pews vary in dimensions, and the effect of well balanced proportion, usually so noticeable in a Gothick church is here totally absent.'
(Cresswell 1924, 195–97).

'Outside the church, built partly in the churchyard, two old cottages now represent what used to be the church ale house, where beer was brewed to refresh worshippers.'
(Bulmer-Thomas 1987, 7).

The plan

The nave and chancel could have stood alone as a classic two-celled church in the Romanesque period (Fernie 2000, fig. 168). But the tower is also visibly early, with its thick walls, plain tower arch, and deeply-splayed window embrasure, and may have formed a component of this early church as well. Whether this was in the 12th or 13th century cannot be precisely determined on the architectural evidence, although the old font, now in Christ Church, certainly indicates a late C12th date for the origin of the church. The misalignment of the tower and nave (see the plan) might be taken as an argument in favour of the tower being an addition.

I think the arcade and east window show the south aisle to be of late 15th or early 16th century date, but the fenestration of the side/south wall ought to be later still (uncusped elliptical-headed lights, straight label moulding, that would be placed in the later 16th century, in domestic contexts). The windows thus offer an outline structural history of the building: deeply splayed window in the tower, possibly late 12th century; the paired lancets of the east window of the chancel, 13th century; the east window of the south aisle, standard Perpendicular tracery of the late 15th or early 16th century; the straight-headed three-light windows with elliptical-headed lights of the north and south walls representing mid.-late 16th century refenestration.

There is evidence of some work in the late 17th century (a date stone of 1685 on the exterior wall of the south aisle), although any work of this date seems too late to relate to the refenestration of the aisle and may not have been extensive enough to appear in the phased plan. There ought also to be an early–mid. C18th phase to cover the furnishings and fittings. The vestry is described as having been 'added to the chancel recently' by James Davidson in 1832, so ought to be keyed as 'late 18th/early 19th century'. (What is the function of the small walk-in space in its north-east corner? Could it possibly be a latrine?)

The [previous] Churches Conservation Trust leaflet has a plan of the building, which is very useful (few such church guides offer a plan), but which is in need of some amendment as to its phasing. The church is shown as two phases; 13th century (tower and chancel), and 15th–16th century (the rest). As just stated I would have thought that body of the church is likely to have a C12th origin, perhaps with additions in the C13th (particularly in the chancel). A little section of the north wall between the tower and first window is also keyed as 13th century on the CCT plan (I did not examine this masonry in detail, but it would seem to be possibly a slip of the pen.)

Historical sources

The church was visited and described by early antiquarian writers, notably Dean Jeremiah Milles, sometime in the mid.-18th century and James Davidson in 1832; a brief description also survives in the Rough Notes of the Exeter Diocesan Architectural Society collected in the 1840s. The parish deposits in the Devon Heritage Centre (DHC) contain two drawings of the interior of the church by J.G. Fuller of c.1850 (DHC P&D 48408). Also available (although not inspected for my lecture) are Churchwardens' accounts from 1712–1803 in the North Devon Record Office and various 20th century minute books and faculty petitions. Much the fullest and most interesting narrative accounts are those of John Stabb, published in 1908 (available on-line: www.wissensdrang.com/dstabb) and Beatrix F. Cresswell's typescript notes on the 'fabric and features of interest' of the church dated 1924). John Stabb's Some Old Devon Churches has the following to say:

'PARRACOMBE. St. Petrock. The church [plate 179a] consists of chancel, nave, south aisle, south porch, and west tower. There were originally three bells, one recast in 1655, another in 1669, and the third in 1743; these bells have been removed to the new church in the village. The oldest parts of the church are Transitional Norman. The chancel is possibly Early English, the south aisle is Perpendicular. The principal object of interest is the screen; this and the screen at Molland are, as far as I know, the only examples we have left in Devonshire of the complete chancel enclosure of the post-Reformation type. The screen [plate 179b] consists of narrow rectangular lights, four on the north side, six on the south of the chancel door; over this is the tympanum filling the chancel arch, on this are hung paintings of the arms of one of the [King] Georges, the Commandments, the Creed, the Lord's Prayer, texts, and the names of Walter Lock and Richard Harton, who were churchwardens in 1758. Mr. Bligh Bond says that in 1780 the rood beam was in existence, and was then cut up for the purpose of making bench-ends, but there is still a beam in situ above the screen which may have been a rood beam. This church is a typical example of what our parish churches looked like a century or more ago [i.e., before 1810]. Here is the old «three-decker» pulpit with sounding board . . . the altar enclosed with rails on three sides, horse-box pews, and raised seats at the west end of the nave for the choir, with holes cut in the pew front for the accommodation of the player of the bass-viol. The Transitional Norman font has been transferred to the new church, and the old church is only used occasionally in the summer months. Unfortunately early in 1908 the church was struck by lightning and much damage done. The tower was cracked, the pulpit and screen split, and the interior of the church almost ruined. The registers date from 1687.' *(Stabb 1908, 100–102).*

Parallels for decoration

Closed tympana – the areas bounded by the lintel of the screen and the chancel arch - were far more common in the 18th century village church than we might now suppose from the few surviving examples (termed 'a speciality of the period' by Pevsner). Other than this one, the best-known surviving example is at Molland, but others are known (for example, the surviving tympanum at Satterleigh in Devon; and a similar structure closing the chancel above the rood beam at Raddington, West Somerset). Formerly there were others at Trentishoe described as 'plain screen with the commandments over' in the EDAS *Rough Notes* of 1847 (Cherry and Pevsner 1989, 876; illustrated in Anon. n.d., XXVIII); at Kentisbury, according to James Davidson which must have gone in the restoration of 1873–74. The EDAS *Rough Notes*, of 1847 say: 'Chancel arch blocked up with tables & arms'. Another example was described by Edmund Rack at Huish Champflower, east of Dulverton in the late 18th century (which also did not survive the 19th century restoration): 'The chancel is separated from the nave by an old open work Gothic screen of five arches, curiously carved and gilded. Over this cornice the upper part of the arch is filled up with the Decalogue and royal arms.' (McDermott and Berry 2011, 363).

Other furnishings

The interior furnishings beautifully represent the liturgical and congregational arrangements of the 18th century village church (Addleshaw and Etchells 1948, chs 3–5; Clarke 1963, chs 2 & 13). The altar rails, around three sides of the altar in a style harking back to the typical 'Laudian' arrangement of the early 17th century, are very plain with stick balusters and simple trefoil heads. (William Laud [1573–1645], made Archbishop of Canterbury by King Charles I in 1633, favoured more Catholic-style ceremony in worship and put rails around the communion table to emphasise its sacred nature. His influences were soon eradicated by the in-coming Puritans after the English Civil War.)

St Petrock's pulpit itself is early 17th century in date, but in its present arrangement is incorporated into a 'three-decker' arrangement of reading desk and clerk's seat, complete with a tester painted with the sun and clouds on a blue-sky background, reminiscent of the much grander scheme of painted representation of the heavens at Muchelney in Somerset (Orbach and Pevsner 2014, 475 and pl. 70). This has an appropriately preachy text from II Corinthians 4:5 painted around the frieze, 'We preach not our selves but Christ Jesus The Lord.' The letter forms of which include the long 's' of the earlier style of 18th century lettering seen elsewhere in the church (below).

Seating is a mixture of 16th or early 17th century benches and 18th century box pews. The former are mainly in the nave and south aisle and display several distinctive features: sill beams laid proud of the floor flags so that one has to step over them to get into the pews; broad and curving sawn boards laid directly on the underlying surface as the base of the pews and shallow 'scratch' mouldings on the edges of the seats.

The interior of the church remains simple and unadorned.

Pews and arches have remained unchanged for congregations down the ages.

The latter have many contemporary carpentry details, H- or H-L hinges, and beautifully crafted top and dado rails of the ramped seating to the west. Some also retain early colouring, possibly graining.

The west end, of course, was traditionally the preserve of the choir and orchestra, either in a gallery or, as in this case, a raised section of seating. The missing panel in one of the pew frontals is said to have served to accommodate the bowing of the bass viol (compare the gallery front at Trentishoe nearby, which has a hole cut for a similar purpose). Readers of Thomas Hardy will be familiar with this tradition from Under the Greenwood Tree (1872) and various short stories (such as 'Absent-mindedness in a Parish Choir' from A Few Crusted Characters of 1891). West Gallery Music – also known as Georgian psalmody – was played in English parish churches and non-Conformist chapels throughout the 18th and most of the 19th centuries, until organs became the pre-eminent church instrument. The recent revival of interest in West Gallery Music also serves to put us in touch with this almost-lost form of church music. The tradition is beautifully represented in Thomas Webster's 1847 painting 'A Village Choir' now in the collection of the Victoria and Albert Museum (a copy of which hangs on the wall in the south aisle at Parracombe).

Painted texts

Texts at Parracombe are painted within moulded oval frames. They are generally in Roman lettering (as opposed to black letter, as is seen in other earlier, 16th and 17th century, examples) and look broadly contemporary with the lettering on the tympanum, which is dated 1758, having broadly similar flourishes, long 's', and the like. I wondered whether the northern panel had been repainted, both because the lettering looks blacker, and it lacks the long 's'. (Although this could be simply the absence of context, one might have expected one such long 's' in 'amongst'.) There are significant differences between the two panels, however, including different mouldings to the frames, which also seem to support a difference in date.

The southern panel has texts from Ecclesiastes 5:1: 'Keep thy foot when thou goest into the house of GOD, and be more ready to hear, than to give the sacrifice of fools: for they consider not that they do evil.' The underlined text is faded to the point of illegibility, perhaps because it was originally in another colour, possibly red. The interesting thing about the choice of this text is that it occurs numerous times in painted texts of the period (inter alia at Bratton Clovelly, Ofwell, and Ugborough in Devon; at Abbey Dore in Herefordshire; at Stokesay in Shropshire, and no doubt in others elsewhere). The second text is from Matthew 21:13: 'My house shall be called the house of prayer.' (omitting the second clause of the verse, which is from the account of the cleansing of the temple, and which continues 'but ye have made it a den of thieves.'!).

The northern cartouche – a carved or cast panel in the form of a scroll - has texts from Exodus 25:8 'Let them make me a Sanctuary, that I may dwell amongst them'; I Chronicles 29:1 'The Palace is not for man but for the Lord God'; and I Corinthians 14:40 'Let all things be done decently and in order'.

The dominant theme here is seemliness in church and God's house. The south panel looks more archaic in lettering style than the inscriptions on the tympanum and the north panel, so it would be reasonable to date this perhaps to the early 18th century, perhaps about 1700, and then the north panel would be contemporary with the cleansing and repainting of the tympanum in 1758. The presence of the scrolly flourishes on the north panel and tympanum, which are absent on the south panel, also suggests that the north panel may be contemporary with the tympanum, but that the south panel is different in date.

Painted texts were a common element in the interior decoration of the churches in the 17th and early 18th centuries (once literacy levels in congregations had reached a sufficient critical mass for such decoration to be viable). There are great examples of near-complete schemes at Bratton Clovelly in Devon (Cherry and Pevsner 1989, 206; Blaylock and Bishop 1993) and Stokesay in Shropshire (Newman and Pevsner 2006, 608–9) and individual panels or surviving fragments of schemes are not uncommon. The artists who produced these works are gradually coming into focus (Davies 2008, 67–70; 89–90; Hamling 2010, 20–21; 106–11). In Devon, the well-known pattern- or sketch-book of the Abbott family of plasterers of Frithelstock, near Great Torrington, has a number of pages devoted to texts in cartouches, strapwork frames and the like.

Several members of the Abbott family served as churchwardens at Frithelstock (and have their names and inscription on bells there: see John Scott et al. 2007, 179). The churchwardens' accounts provide specimens of their handwriting which help in identifying the different hands at work in the sketchbook as recent research by Dr Jenny Saunt has shown (Saunt 2021). Accounts also mention painting texts, for example John Abbott of Southcott the younger (1642–88) records payments to himself for 'writing on the church walls' (NDRO 3788A/PO/1/1, 1650–72; 3788A/PW/1/1, 1695–1767). That craftsmen principally known for their plasterwork had a sideline in making such painted decoration represents a significant insight into the processes by which this work was carried out.

The Monuments

There are two medieval cross slabs in the church: one in front of the altar, placed south of John Newell's ledger slab; this is a trapezoidal, or coffin-shaped, stone with an incised floriated cross, and is said to mark the tomb of a medieval priest (Cresswell 1924, 200). The second is re-used as the threshold of the south doorway. This is a smaller slab, with a cross raised in relief. There appears to be the remains of one floriated terminal surviving to the west; in the middle the relief decoration is entirely worn away by foot traffic, but remains of the cross shaft survive towards the base of the stone to the east.

Two wall monuments either side of the south door are to members of the Lock family from Rowley, which is part of the parish. They are made of painted timber and feature attractive graining and marbling (an overlooked art of helping poorer materials to look better) dating from the late 18th century, 1786–1803. There is also marbling on the third monument in the south aisle (to Walter Lock, d. 1732, and several other family members). The mid.-18th century monument in the chancel is interesting for the false masonry jointing, imitating ashlar, painted on the surround of the niche, another way of improving the appearance of basic materials.

Other Details

There are many minor features to intrigue and delight in the church, including the fragments of blind traceried panels built into the base of the tower

Church-goers had rudimentary seating.

buttresses, which testify to lost late medieval architectural ornament. There's an incised daisy wheel in the hollow moulding on the south-east face of the first pier of the arcade from the west, plus the remains of another above it. Properly described as apotropaic, these were supposed to have the power to avert evil. And there's other graffiti throughout the church with the initial CG cut into the west jamb of the south door and various names and initials cut into the rear pews.

The ubiquitous hat pegs around the walls reflect a time when nobody was without a hat (and remind us of how different our age is from theirs). The iron door handle is worth a mention, as are the monuments in the chancel (see the elephant heads on the shield of the Newell ledger slab and the floriated cross mentioned already). The Lock monuments in the south aisle have nice relief-carved details (a scallop shell, winged putti and the like).

This church is special both for its intact early fabric and for its survival of pre-ecclesiological furnishings and interior arrangement, as well as for some individual star points of the fittings and furnishings.

Ruskin and Parracombe

by Meriel O'Dowd

Meriel works for the Churches Conservation Trust, looking after the fabric of 118 churches and 40 churchyards spread over 12 counties in the West. In her spare time she's a Guardian of the Society for the Protection of Ancient Buildings (SPAB)and runs their Somerset Regional group. This church embodies the crossover between these two organisations, both at times desperately trying to stop these buildings being demolished for the last 150 years.

John Ruskin

On 8th February 1819, at No.54, Hunter Street, Brunswick Square, in between the Foundling Hospital and the British Museum, John Ruskin was born.

A quick internet search brings up a vast amount of information, with him being described thus:

'John Ruskin was the leading English art critic of the Victorian era, as well as an art patron, draughtsman, watercolourist, a prominent social thinker and philanthropist. He wrote on subjects as varied as geology, architecture, myth, ornithology, literature, education, botany and political economy.'

An only child, home schooled until the age of 14, his parents were a huge influence on him with his mother's lessons, his father's literary and artistic tastes and the annual Ruskin family summer tour which often lasted months. This started as tours of the Lake District, which profoundly influenced his love of vernacular architecture and craftsmanship, but by the summer of 1833, when Ruskin was 14, they set out on tours of the continent, the first of which followed a route from Dover to Calais, then on to Strasbourg by following the Rhine, through the Alps to Switzerland and Italy taking in Milan, Genoa and Turin then back through the Alps to Interlaken and Chamonix and back to England via Paris.

He constantly sketched and wrote poetry on this tour which resulted in his first published work aged 15 entitled 'On the Causes of the colour of the Rhine' in London's magazine of natural history.

Ruskin visited Venice for the first time aged 16, and it was European tours that formed the basis of his writing on architecture and conservation, as it seemed each time he went back, he saw more of his beloved ancient architecture demolished. Whilst at university in Oxford, Ruskin wrote a series of essays which formed the book 'The Poetry of Architecture', published decades later with the alternative title 'The Architecture of the Nations of Europe considered in its association with natural scenery and national character'.

On his tours of Yorkshire, the Lake District and the Derbyshire Dales, Ruskin found himself looking at the vernacular cottage architecture and the following year contrasted this with domestic architecture on his tour of Scotland.

In 1845, when he was 26, Ruskin made his first European trip without his parents, and it was in Lucca in Italy that we see his first impassioned diary entries on the destruction he saw at the church of San Frediano.

He wrote: 'Such a church – so old – 680 probably –

all glorious dark arches & columns – covered with holy frescoes – and gemmed gold pictures on blue grounds. I don't know when I shall get away, and all the church fronts charged with heavenly sculpture and inlaid with whole histories in marble – only half of them have been destroyed by the Godless, soulless, devil hearted and brutebrained barbarians … one sees nothing but subjects for lamentation, wrecks of lovely things destroyed, remains of them unrespected, all going to decay.'

He filled his notebooks with sketches of churches, teaching himself Gothic architecture, tracing and copying frescoes before they decayed or were destroyed to make way for new tombs and monuments. He often worked feverishly from 5 o'clock in the morning to mid evening, paying for scaffolding to be erected allowing him better access and writing back to his worried father that 'the scaffold was safe, he drank only clean water and he would eat no figs!' The letters he wrote home were filled with rage at the probable fate of the wall paintings in Lucca, Pisa and Florence.

He saw both at home and abroad the destruction that was being wrought on medieval architecture. At home, Augustus Welby Northmore Pugin had published his first book 'Contrasts' in 1836, highlighting the neglect and destruction of medieval churches in England, followed in 1841 by 'The True Principles of Pointed or Christian architecture'. On the one hand, Pugin attacked the destruction of buildings such as Salisbury Cathedral where 'the venerable bell tower… [was pulled down as well as] the Hungerford and Beauchamp chapels … and a host of other barbarities too numerous to recite' yet, on the other hand, he writes that churches needed to be adapted to the requirements of the Protestant faith. Pugin was concerned with churches fulfilling his idea and understanding 'the true principles' of the traditional form and arrangement of a church.

Also at home, following the ideas of Pugin, the Cambridge Camden Society, which was later renamed the Ecclesiological Society, was founded in 1839. In

Parracombe Church, near Lynton, N. Devon.

P. N. LEAKEY, RECTOR.

UNDER THE PATRONAGE OF
SIR THOMAS AND LADY ACLAND,
SIR WILLIAM AND LADY MUIR,
LADY ANNA LOFTUS,
PROFESSOR RUSKIN,
THE REV. E. CAPEL CURE, RECTOR OF ST. GEORGE, HANOVER SQUARE,
AND SEVERAL MEMBERS OF THE SOCIETY FOR THE PROTECTION OF ANCIENT BUILDINGS.

A FANCY SALE

Will be held at No. 17, Stratford Place, Oxford Street, W., on 2nd and 3rd July, 1878, in aid of the funds for building a new Parish Church at Parracombe, and preserving the old one (which dates from the 12th century), for use as a Mortuary Chapel.

This Sale will include a collection of Indian, Chinese and other Curiosities and Works of Art.

By the kind permission of the owners, there will be on View a valuable collection of Oil Paintings by Gainsborough, Turner, Sir Peter Lely, Sir J. Reynolds, Stodard, R. A. Dante, G. Rosetti, Le Gros, Millais' Pen and Ink Sketch from which he painted his famous picture of 'The Carpenters Shop.' Mr. Holman Hunt has also kindly consented to add two drawings recently made by him in Palestine, and his corrected proof engraving of 'The Scapegoat.'

Refreshments will be provided.

The Sale will commence at noon each day. Admission, One Shilling.

Please bring your friends.

P.T.O.

'A Fancy Sale' was organised to help save St Petrock's.

Reverend Leakey's letter supporting Parracombe's new church.

the same year, the Oxford Architectural and Historical Society was also founded. Many restoration architects including George Street, William Butterfeld and George Gilbert Scott were influenced by its principles. Churches had to be restored back to their former glory.

So in the 1840's in England, a new debate began dividing people into restorers and anti-restorationists. On the one hand, the restorers were concerned with ensuring that a restoration was faithful to the original building, and on the other, the anti-restorationalists did not focus on the significance of the oldest known phase of the building and try to fake it back to that but valued each layer as specific to its historic and cultural context each with the same level of significance and campaigned to protect and conserve authentic historic building fabric of all ages.

In 1849, Ruskin published 'The Seven Lamps of Architecture'. Hidden right at the end of the lamp of memory, in sections 18, 19 and 20, Ruskin focuses on the three concepts of:

- restoration as destruction,
- maintenance and
- the revolutionary concept that we are only guardians of historic buildings for future generations. (All of which would be taken up 28 years later by William Morris in his manifesto.)

Ruskin describes restoration as 'the most total destruction which a building can suffer' and states 'it is impossible, as impossible as to raise the dead to restore anything that has been great or beautiful in architecture…that spirit which is given only by the hand and eye of the workman never can be recalled. Another spirit may be given by another time but then it is a new building but the spirit of the dead workman cannot be summoned up.' So here we see the ideas of authenticity of fabric and the value of workmanship explored.

Next up is maintenance, and he states 'the principle of modern times … is to neglect buildings first and restore them afterwards.' And as there are no charitable funds for maintenance this principle could be said to still apply today. Ruskin advises us to 'put a few sheets of lead on the roof, clear out dead leaves and sticks from a water course, watch with anxious care, count its stones as you would jewels of a crown,

…'bind it together with iron where it loosens, stay it with timber where it declines; do not care about the unsightliness of the aid; better a crutch than a lost limb and do this tenderly and reverently and continually.'

Added to this was the revolutionary idea that he furthered; that ancient buildings are common and not private property (which was encapsulated later in Morris' statement that 'We are only trustees for those that come after us'). This wouldn't be officially accepted until the mid-20th century (post-World War Two planning acts), by which time it was implied in international conservation charters.

By the time Ruskin came to write his preface to the 1880 edition, he wrote 'the buildings I described with so much delight [are now] either knocked down or scraped and patched up into smugness and smoothness more tragic than uttermost ruin.'

Four years later he published 'The Stones of Venice' and he continues these themes peppering his descriptions of St Mark's and other places with phrases decrying modern restorers who have 'destroyed fringes of mosaic flower work' in St Mark's and so on.

Ruskin's contribution to the founding of the Society for the Protection of Ancient Buildings

At the opening of the re-sited Crystal Palace in Sydenham, Ruskin made a speech, calling for the founding of a society to protect these ancient buildings.

This lit a flame in William Morris. He would later meet and establish a close friendship with Ruskin. He and Edward Burne-Jones, a Pre-Raphaelite artist, became more and more annoyed by the academic-led restoration.

In 1874, Morris signed the petition against replacing the Georgian tower of St. John's church in Hampstead with one in the Gothic style. In that year, too, Ruskin refused to accept the Royal Institute of British Architect's Gold Medal citing that his refusal was because so many historic buildings and so much art was being destroyed all over Europe in the name of 'restoration'. Meanwhile restoration works to cathedrals and churches in England had become commonplace big business.......Restoration works to Burford church angered William Morris, which he saw while en route to see friends, with whom he then discussed the matter and what they could do.

What Morris saw at Tewkesbury Abbey resulted in him writing an open letter to the Athenaeum in 1877 in which he calls for the setting up of a body to keep watch on old monuments. A fortnight later Morris, Webb and 15 of their friends met at Morris' house where they formally constituted the Society for the Protection of Ancient Buildings and its manifesto. This was widely reported in the newspapers as would be their weekly meetings thereafter. Ruskin sent a letter of support and afterwards sat on the committee.

Together, they presented a formidable combination of consistent doctrine, scholarly resource and lobbying skills and, though the Society of Antiquaries had intervened in a few cases before 1877, the SPAB was the first conservation organisation whose sole purpose was to lobby and campaign for the protection of the built historic environment. But it took several more years of campaigning before any legislation was passed by the government to back this up.

Ruskin's contribution to saving St Petrock's church

On September 20th 1877, in response to the publication of the SPAB's manifesto, a letter was received by Ruskin from high on Exmoor, in deepest, darkest Devon, from a Reverend Peter Nettleton Leakey of Parracombe.

He wrote:

My Dear Sir,

I believe that you are connected with the Anti-Church restoration society and therefore will, I am sure, assist me in very arduous work that I am trying to do....I was very grieved on coming here to find an old church of the 12th century almost in ruins. For a long time I hardly knew what to do as I am a poor man with a large family and there are no people in the Parish to assist me.

I was anxious to preserve the old church and consulted an Architect. He said that it was in such a ruinous condition that I should be obliged to pull it down. The church is most inconveniently situated on the top of the hill a long way off from the people.

I proposed therefore to my Parishioners to repair the church sufficiently to keep it from falling and to use it as a mortuary chapel and that I would build a new one in the village among the people.

After a great deal of opposition I have carried my point but I have to find nearly the whole money required - £3,000. I have collected £2,000 but nowhere to get the balance.

By saving this church I shall keep a very interesting relic. The east end window is unique. There is only one other of its kind in England. There is a most interesting carved rood screen and some of the seats are very old of massive thick oak.

I was told by a friend that your society would approve of my proceedings.

Various letters were exchanged with Leakey emphasizing his large family each time: 'my people are poor, we have no gentry and I have a small means with so many sons to educate!' and requesting the names and addresses of the SPAB membership so he could appeal for funds. 'It seems to me that the best way in which your committee could assist me would be by giving me a strong letter of approval which I would have printed and send to every member of your society a copy but it would be well if each member of your committee would give me a small donation.'

(Research reveals there were three sons in the Leakey family: Charles, Percy and Alexander.)

Ruskin wrote back:

My Dear Sir,

I enclose a cheque for ten pounds and only wish it were in my power to send more, in order to show my respect for you as the first clergyman known to me who has seen the right way and, far more, taken it in this quite limitless and important matter.

Faithfully and gratefully yours, J. Ruskin.

More correspondence ensues with mention of Rev. Leakey attending the SPAB annual meeting, and then Leakey hits on another way that Ruskin could help him and writes:

May I suggest a new way in which your society can help me by assisting me in a bazaar which I propose to hold next May or June in London. I want the loan of a room in the West end of London for 2 days. Also, some person of position to patronise it. Do try and help me in this. I shall be very glad of any contributions to the bazaar.

Amazingly, as we can see from the pamphlet advertising the ensuing event, Ruskin set to and organised his friends to both patronise the event and also to donate items to be displayed and sold.

The pamphlet reads:

A Fancy Sale will be held at No.17 Stratford Place, Oxford Street W., on 2nd and 3rd July, 1878, in aid of the funds for building a new Parish church at Parracombe, and preserving the old one. The sale will include a collection of Indian, Chinese and other curiosities and works of art. By kind permission of the owners, there will be on view, a valuable collection of oil paintings by Gainsborough, Turner, Sir Peter Lely, Sir Joshua Reynolds, Stodard, R.A.Dante, G.Rosetti, Le Gros, Millais' pen and ink sketch from which he painted The Carpenter's Shop.

Mr Holman Hunt has also kindly consented to add two drawings recently made by him in Palestine, and his corrected proof engraving of 'The Scapegoat'.

Refreshments will be provided.

The sale will commence at noon each day. Admission one shilling.

Bring your friends.

As he had been collecting Turner paintings for years, we can assume that Ruskin himself lent these and asked friends from the Pre-Raphaelite brotherhood to put forward their paintings. A description in 1877 of Ruskin's house, Brantwood by Alexander Wedderburn mentions:

'a lovely maid from Gainsborough's easel, 4 Turners and a painting of Rosamund by Burne-Jones.'

Rather than just putting his name to the Fancy Sale, we know that Ruskin must have actively approached his friends and asked them to help because the first people mentioned are Sir Thomas and Lady Acland. These are the mother and father of Ruskin's best friend at university, Henry Acland, who was one of Ruskin's lifelong friends. Conveniently, the Acland estates were in Devon so they were an obvious choice.

Sir Thomas was a British educational reformer and politician, and patron of the Arts, so as his London house was a nine minute walk from the fancy sale ,I'd like to think that he lent paintings too. Family estates at Holnicote in Somerset and Killerton in Devon were later donated to the National Trust.

The next people on the list are Sir William and Lady Muir. Sir William Muir was a Scottish orientalist and colonial administrator serving as Principal of the University of Edinburgh and Lieutenant Governor of the North West Provinces of India. The Fancy Sale leaflet states 'The sale will include a collection of Indian, Chinese and other Curiosities and Works of Art' and it is tempting to think that Sir William contributed at least the Indian curiosities to be sold in aid of Parracombe.

Lady Anna Loftus and the Rev E Capel Cure complete the list of patrons along with Ruskin.

The back of the leaflet explains why Parracombe is so important, appealing to the widespread antiquarian feeling in the nineteenth century.

The SPAB's 142 year involvement in Parracombe

Temporarily saved by Ruskin and Leakey, St Petrock's was not yet out of difficulties. In 1908 the church was struck by lightning. This was one of several occasions when the SPAB offered further advice about the building's care during the 20th century.

St Petrock's was severely damaged by lightning and in true media style it was sensationalised with 'pieces of masonry weighing several hundred weight were hurled hundreds of feet away, the pulpit was shattered and it has sustained almost irreparable damage' - but repair it they did.

Thackeray Turner, SPAB secretary, wrote to Lethaby, an architect, who asked Alfred H. Powell, an architect who lived at Barrington Court (now another National trust property, this time in Somerset) to survey the damaged church, and he estimates the damage at £160 and, using Leakey's proven method of an appeal to the public backed by the SPAB, the funds were raised.

In 1971, like William Morris's beloved church at Inglesham in Wiltshire, St Petrock's, Parracombe became one of the first churches to be vested in the Redundant Churches Fund (now the Churches Conservation Trust).

Vesting repairs were carried out by the Bristol Architect John Keeling Maggs and included quite major repairs to the south aisle wall and the leaning Nave arcade.

The Churches Conservation Trust has strong links with the SPAB and follows the same minimal intervention repair philosophy backed up with twice yearly maintenance visits. This philosophy is aided by us not having much money to do anything anyway!

In 2007 my predecessor, Brian Clark, led a campaign of repairs over two years to try to sort out the damp at the west end of the church with John Bucknall, architect and SPAB scholar. They used Carrek as a contractor and spent days and days flushing out the tower masonry with clean water which had to be carried from the local streams in bowsers to the top of the tower. The original lime bedding mortar had presumably had a high earth content as is usual, and centuries of water penetration had washed this out leaving enormous voids, so the tower masonry was acting as a header tank leading to a beautiful fernery with green mould living on the interior walls of the tower and creeping up the columns. The interior was repointed first and then 15% of the volume of the tower was allowed in pozzolanic grout which is pumped in under pressure. This was all used up when only two fifths of the way up the tower, and the church was left for a year so that it could all settle and the lime could go off. In the next summer, the tower grouting was completed and the merlons stabilised. Working for the CCT we get the opportunity to take the long view and undertake these works gently phasing them over a number of years and not having to cram them all into one rushed project.

In 2017, one of the panels in the nave cracked and fell. We put up a scaffold to repair it with Simon Cartlidge, architect & SPAB scholar, and Devon contractors Williams & Burroughs. Whilst the repair was relatively simple, gaining access to this high level allowed us to glimpse the bright reds, blues and yellows underneath the white limewash which has probably covered the ceiling since the seventeenth century, offering us a tantalising glimpse of its once brightly coloured interior.

And, as we're minimal intervention anti-scrape

philosophy, I'm afraid that's all you're ever going to see of the coloured Medieval decoration in this church! Blame Ruskin!

In conclusion, I hope I have demonstrated what a significant figure John Ruskin was in forming why we venerate and save ancient buildings today and the conservation philosophy that we use to justify and design interventions.

The way we see old buildings in Britain, and value them as the work of those that went before us, value their patina and their historical layers, can be seen to have come from what Ruskin said and wrote.

We know of many incidences when Ruskin wrote letters and gave advice about buildings but, to my knowledge, St Petrock's, Parracombe is a unique example of where he actively got involved, appealing to his friends and fundraising to save the historic fabric of the building.

His huge influence is still with us every day in our care and repair of the beautiful venerable structures that we are merely guardians of and, in the casework that the SPAB undertake, campaigning to save what is left.

Ruskin helped change the thinking on church renovation.

The Man Who Made the Gravestones

by Bob Godfrey

William Watts was a school teacher, registrar, garden and headstone engraver – and you can see plenty of examples of his handiwork if you look around the graveyard at St Petrock's. He bequeathed his family two books that contained diary entries and accounts, giving us a sideways glance at his life and times. Bob Godfrey has made a study of the diary and here, outlines links with St Petrock's Church.

In an indenture of 1852 William describes himself as 'Schoolmaster, Land-surveyor, and Engraver'. With more than one string to his bow, he arrived in Parracombe, with other skills and capabilities well

established before he took up his post in the school. The fact that he was literate and numerate, in ways that the local farmers may not have been, gave him an important role in surveying and recording in the community. He measured land, kept records of the bidders at farm sales and was meticulous in cataloguing his own smallholder produce – in particular his meticulous records of potato planting and harvest. All these activities demonstrate William's busy involvement in village life beyond the confines of the school. The church was also important to him. He attended regularly, commented on sermons he heard and, on occasion, deputised for the Parish Clerk at weddings and funerals.

Typically, Watts left his name at the bottom of gravestones and a distinctive emblem at the top.

As an engraver, we are immediately struck by the extent of the village schoolmaster's work in producing gravestones for an incredibly wide community. The Large Book suggests that over 20 years he provided gravestones to at least a dozen or more villages round about - Parracombe and Berrynarbor and Combe Martin you might expect, but also to Marwood, Lynton, Arlington, Pilton, Charles, and more. He created or restored about a dozen or so a year and the prices he charged varied according to the extent of the work. There is an early account of 1846 which gives a good idea of the work entailed:

'Jan 1846 Rd Harton's mother's gravestone Ac/t:

Cleaning the stone etc.	1s/6d
3 layers best black paint	1s/6d
for Painting the ornament & border	1s/6d
Painting 21 words (old work) at 1d per word	1s/9d
Engraving & painting 29 new words at 3d a word	7/3d
Total	13s/6d'

Here he was working on an established gravestone in situ. The fact that gravestones were painted is interesting and that they were 'serviced', ie cleaned and repainted. Over twenty years, William must have produced well over 100 new stones and engraved for one or two or more people like the one for Martha Polkinghorne which he erected August 3rd, 1850, for £1.5s.

This stone is decorated in each corner with what looks like lilies, the inscription is surrounded with flourishes, and he uses italic script, capitals and roman lettering. He also has, as he always did, placed his name in a dominant position on the stone - an important way of self advertising. He used a range of other motifs including urns, leaves, crosses and the like. His fresh stones came mainly from a quarry in Combe Martin and he would often pick up stones in response to an order, but then he would take one or two extra which he recorded as 'in speculation'. It saved him a journey, perhaps, in a borrowed cart (he didn't own one) and at the same time it meant that he was always ready to answer the need - and in 19th century England he was rarely without this work. On average, it earned him about £2.00 a stone and there cannot be a graveyard within about a fifteen mile radius from Parracombe that hasn't an example of his work. Parracombe itself has plenty.

He also erected stones for one member of a family but engraved in such a way that further names could be added at a later date. This was clearly the case with the stone erected for John and Betty Harding which began with the death of their first son Richard who died in 1793, when the child was 8 months old, and 10 years before William was born. You could say that it began life as a memorial to a long lost child. But, in the end, the tombstone told the whole family history surrounding one marriage between John and Betty Harding who outlived most of their own children and one grandchild. Their own deaths are recorded at the bottom of the stone.

To the Memory of
RICHARD HARDING, the Son of JOHN
And BETTY HARDING of Trentishoe late of
this Parish. He died on14th day of August
1793 Aged 8 months
Also to the Memory of MARIA HARDING his
Sister, who died at Bristol on the 19th day of April
1822, aged 25 years
Also to the Memory of HENRY HARDING her
Brother who died on 17th March 1834
Aged 27 years.
Also to the Memory of REBECCA HARDING his
Sister who died on 3rd day of October 1838,
Aged 26 years
Also to the Memory of CHARITY HARDING her
Sister who died on 10th day of August 1842
Aged 26 years
Also to the memory of ANNA MARIA HARDING
Daughter of WILLIAM and HARRIET HARDING
She died on 15th day of August 1842
Aged 9 years
Also to the memory of HENRY HARDING
Who died on 15th day of February 1853 Aged 1 year
Also to the Memory of BETTY HARDING
Who died on 25th day of January 1854
Aged 81 years
Also to the Memory of JOHN HARDING
Who died on 26th day of April 1854
Aged 93 years.

The stone William Watts put up in December 1848 at a cost of two pounds, five shillings and eight pence remains a silent witness to the nature of life and death for a family in a 19th century village.

Speaking of this question of death in the village and thereabouts - when William was 54 in 1857, the role of Registrar for Births and Deaths for the Parracombe district came up due to the death of Thomas Baker of Lynton, the then incumbent. William had worked for Mr Baker in the years before, counting the populations in the Parracombe district and seems to have harboured a serious ambition to do the job of registrar. He knew that his old rival Charles Blackmore, master of a competing school and a Wesleyan, was also interested, something to make William even more intent perhaps on securing the post. In the Large Book, we read that a week before the interview for the job he went to Barum to canvass members of the Board of Guardians. His entry for 26th June reveals his true feelings about it:

'26 June, 1857, I attended the board of guardians Barnstaple as a candidate for the office of registrar of births and deaths for the Parracombe district, comprising Brendon, Countisbury, Challacombe, High Bray, Lynton, Martinhoe, Parracombe & Trentishoe. Candidates William Watts, Parracombe, Charles Blackmore, Parracombe. William Baker not being eligible the contest lay between Wm.W and C.B. When WW was returned by a large majority - WW 16 votes and C.B. only 7 a majority for W.Watts of 9 - triumphant!'

There was a report in the following week's North Devon Journal which suggested that the meeting had been unusually well attended on this occasion by Church of England representatives on the Board. We have to suspect that William's canvassing had alerted some of the otherwise sleeping members of the Board to another threat from Chapel.

A further hint of his keenness for the post may be found in the Book where he records that his appointment came through from London two days later on 28th June, and he went directly to Lynton to 'get the iron box, books and documents from Mr Baker in Lynton.' He set to work immediately making his first registrations on 4th July of births in Parracombe and Martinhoe and a death in High Bray on the 6th. On 7th July 'I put a board up against the front of my house with the words 'W.Watts registrar of births and deaths for the Parracombe district'. He made his first visits on 11th July to Challacombe, High Bray and Trentishoe and to Brendon, Countisbury, Lynton and Martinhoe on 18th. On the 24th, the Board of Guardians approved his appointment of Mr P. Dovell as his deputy. Thus he was launched into a new career at the age of 54, and two further entries in the Book point to a clear sense that he felt it gave him higher status than his school teaching.

'12th September, 1858, The Inspector of registration, Edward Edwards Esq from Somerset House, London, came here to inspect my books and said that I was an excellent registrar and my books done credit and that I should make one of the best.'

A few months later he writes: '12th February, 1859, Was at Barum with my certified copies, Mr.Barry, Superintendent Registrar passed most excellent.'

Furthermore, like his engraving work, the job got him out more frequently into the wider community of Exmoor and beyond.

Speaking then of William and births and deaths, I would like to go on to consider his role as family man, a factor that features in the Large Book and whose significance it is perhaps easy to overlook. He arrived in Parracombe in 1841 as husband to Maria and father of Mary aged 9, William junior, sometimes called Bill, aged 6, Phillip aged 3 and Maria, the baby, aged 1. Their fifth and last child, Martha, was born and christened in Parracombe in 1842. From this time through to 1848, his recording of family life is spasmodic but often revealing. For instance, in May 1841, soon after settling into Parracombe, he took Mary and William back to Berrynarbor presumably to see their grandfather and aunts and uncles in the area. At the end of May 'father came to see us', 'stopped to Tuesday morn' and when he came to leave, William walked with his father to 'the west end of Dean Down'. This exchange between Berrynarbor and Parracombe continues on and off and quite regularly with different members of the family walking or riding there. In the year 1847, for example, when they were 14 and 12 years old respectively, first Mary on 5th April, and then William on 20th April, went on their own to Berrynarbor and each stayed over for 3 days. That to me shows remarkably confident parents allowing them to journey, it seems quite alone, along that route. They knew, of course, that they would be well cared for once they arrived in Berrynarbor. There are also records of family outings to the Valley of Rocks, walking there and back on the same day. As I said, these occasions were recorded spasmodically in amongst all the other things that William was engaged with. Nevertheless, it does convey a sense of a well functioning family.

Nowhere is this more poignantly expressed than in William's extraordinary account of his wife Maria's death in January 1848. First of all, the story stands out because it is an extended piece of prose suddenly appearing in the midst of the terse, rather blunt, diary entries. Its detail is painfully evocative of the moments surrounding Maria's passing. The scene is set with his account of Maria's long illness and her growing weakness. It is evening. The little ones, Maria (8) and Martha (6) are put to bed. Mary, William and

Phillip remain to take part in family prayers, in which Maria joins. Then the boys go to bed leaving Mary and William to minister to Maria. All of this leaves us with an indelible impression of a loving and close family undoubtedly belonging together through their religious practice. The account that follows of Maria's final moments is almost unbearable to read; it is so literal, direct, tactile and tender. We are present in the moment and made sensitive to the keen sense of loss that William himself felt. Immediately after Maria has died the family group is reassembled: 'the other dear children, viz the boys, were come down and to hear the cries and lamentations of the dear little lambs was enough to rend the stoutest heart'. 'Lord have mercy', he prays, 'upon me and my dear children she was a good and virtuous wife and tender mother.'

[Maria was not buried at St Petrock's but at Berrynarbour, where she was born.] Thus it was that from January 1848 William began life as a single parent with five children, a matter that must have played upon his mind. He thought often I'm sure about the possibility of marrying again and nowhere is this more evident than in a note he made along the margin of the page on which he had meticulously recorded the expenses of Maria's funeral. He wrote:

'February 2nd, 1848, Mrs.Saml. Charley died leaving five children
February 4th, 1848, Mrs.Jn Hill died leaving five children'
John Hill married again within six months
Saml Charley married again February 5th 1849 exactly the day 12 month that he buried his first wife.'

Thus William records the experience of two men left in the same predicament as himself and appears to be reflecting on the timing of their remarriages. He himself took his time and married Agnes Jones of Highley, in October 1850, two years and ten months after Maria died. With regard to this marriage, my curiosity has been aroused by an entry in the School Accounts section for June 1841 which records:

Agnes Jones four weeks 2s

In all the Accounts it's the only entry for that particular name and leads me to propose that it was the same Agnes Jones. Thus, supposing Agnes was a pupil in 1841 and being of 'just age' in 1850, as the marriage certificate has it, she will perhaps have been about 21 at the time of the wedding. That may account for any delay in coming to that decisive moment. It might also account for the slightly coy way in which William enters the events around his marriage in the Large Book:

'14 September, 1850, Revd JD made tea for me and Mr R and made me a present of a £ to buy the L & O (ie the Licence and the ring).
'30 September, At the Reverend Munday's direction for a marriage licence £3.0s 0d…'
'19 October, Married by the Reverend John Pyke, rector.'

Followed by later entry also dated 19 October:

'Mr Watts and Miss Jones married at Parracombe.'

Was it significant that Mary, the eldest daughter, a month after the wedding, went off into service with a Mr Scamp of Ilfracombe at a penny a week? There is little clue about that but what we do know is that she was within two days of her 18th birthday when she finally moved away from the family, with William's blessing: 'Poor dear Mary,… may God bless prosper and protect her and all of us in this life…'

How does history judge William Watts? He was a slightly disenchanted teacher but a man of religious conviction who in everything did his work with diligence and left his mark in stones and Registers and in his Large and Small Books, to a posterity that reads those books with keen interest and much pleasure and has come to appreciate him in ways I think he would thoroughly have enjoyed.

On the Record

Several surviving books have helped furnish details for this new account of St Petrock's. Already mentioned, the 1917 edition of the Devon & Cornwall Record Society book has been illuminating, as has the 1918 copy of Dwelly's Parish Records, not least because, between them, the births, marriages and deaths register and the headstone inscriptions are transcribed into modern, printed English. Of course, mistakes may have been made in the transcription which might yet come to light.

Chanter reveals the principal inhabitants of Parracombe at the time parish registers first started in 1538, when Thomas Cromwell said that every wedding, baptism and burial should be recorded. (Administrative records got a lot more durable when parchment was used instead of paper.) Records from the era were characteristically in Latin and difficult to read. After 1558, the records were kept in a chest for safe keeping, alongside other local governance notes. In 1597 – the earliest dates recorded in Chanter's book – a second copy had to be devised for each church's bishop although it's acknowledged that these were not always complete.

The richest man in Tudor times appears to have been John Harrey of Rowley, with John Berry at Middleton and John Thorne of 'Tokinmyll' also listed.

The first baptism on the register, dated 1597, relates to Priscilla being christened, the illegitimate daughter of 'one Marie, a stranger'. Three days later Anne Steere was baptised, recorded as the daughter of Joan Steere. Was this another illegitimate child or a relation of John Steere, the first burial listed that same year?

Other burials that feature on this early register include those of William Sherwill, Egline Squire, Anne Harnatte, Margaret Rooke and John Burgess. But while the records of their passing remains in print, their graves have long since disappeared from view.

There were no weddings in 1597 so the first recorded in this register is between Peter Smith and Agnes Thorn on 29 April 1598.

Chanter notes that, while the names of the era recurred in the records for a few decades, there was a steady exit and influx of agricultural workers.

'Very few of the families stayed more than four or five generations in the parish and this tendency is still going on,' Chanter wrote. 'At the present day there are not more than three or four families residing in the parish who have been in it for more than five generations.'

The reasons he gave was the manors in Parracombe – Rowley, Middleton and Parracombe Mill – were not ruled by an influential squire but the site of several freehold farms. Also, the generous amount of common grazing land offered to labourers a route out of poverty and on to small farms. The desire to better themselves then took them to pastures new. And names that crop up frequently in the earliest of the records, like Bagbeer, Juell, Larimore, Cunnibeer, do fade from view.

The transcripts between 1635 and 1662 are missing, an era that included the English Civil War. It's not known whether the church was spared or punished by the victorious Parliamentarians. The next set of records are indecipherable or missing so the names that appear when John Blackmore was rector include the more familiar Dovells, Locks, Blackmores, Gammons, Crangs and Roachs. The last recorded burial in the register relates to Richard Nicholls of Parracombe Mill, who was buried on 20 December 1836, aged 74.

Vestry Minutes

A transcription of the Vestry minutes between 1813 and 1856 is held by the village's history group, revealing how a group of leading citizens sometimes met monthly, but often only sporadically, to deal with parish business. The Vestry, as it was known, provided governance for the village. Names that appear on its pages are also in the churchyard at St Petrock's. The descriptions of the meetings are tantalisingly brief and there's no record of the discussions before resolutions were made.

The committee apparently met to conduct its business which included appointing church wardens, setting the poor rate (a tax levied on property in each parish to provide help for the poor), maintaining roads and repairing the church itself.

However, the minutes tell us that there was a meeting held on 6 January 1813 – during the Napoleonic Wars - to consult about the raising of volunteers for the local militia. Those attending were Richard Blackmore, John Gammin, John Blackmore and P Tucker. For some years, vestry meetings were held at the Fox and Goose Inn – a thatched building described as 'old and low' by Arthur Smyth in 1876 - an indication perhaps that the church was already an relatively inhospitable venue.

In 1814, a Vestry meeting at the Fox and Goose Inn on 10 October, had the repair of the church floor as the main the topic of discussion. And that wasn't the only expense facing the parish, which wanted to buy a new Common Prayer Book for the minister as well as construct a gate for the churchyard. From this distance, it's impossible to tell which gate was installed.

Later that decade, meetings were held about who should repair the roads, with John Crang, Philip Tucker, William Dovell, Richard Lovering and William and Richard Roach putting their names forward for the task.

On 3 April 1820, once again at the Fox and Goose, there was general agreement promoting Sunday school and footing the bill for 'the weekly instruction of six poor children'.

Ten years after that, it was resolved the sum of £15 should be taken from the church rate in order to build a vestry room in the churchyard, worth something in the region of £1,725 today. Those present for the meeting were chairman Rev Pyke, William Dovell, James Smyth, John Crang, John Harding, David Lock Roach, Richard Lovering and Philip Dovell.

Six parish constables to oversee public order were appointed in 1844. According to vestry minutes the men were George Smyth, John Gammin, John Lock Roach, Nathaniel Dovell, William Harding and Henry Monk or Moule. The following year, Henry was replaced by John Blackmore who himself also lasted only a year. Later, William Watts would join the ranks of the constables in Parracombe.

In August 1846, there was a meeting to consult about the repair and widening of the road between Bodley Cross and Parracombe Mill. The committee got together again in the depths of December to appeal against an order made by Barnstaple magistrates 'for the removal of Susan Blackmore, singlewoman, and her two bastard children from the parish of Barnstaple to the parish of Parracombe'. With rector John Pyke in the chair, it was unanimously resolved to employ one Mr Bray 'or some other competent person' to make the appeal, the results of which are at present unknown.

On 17 April 1850, William Slader was appointed sexton, with responsibilities including the chiming of the bells twice daily and cleaning the church inside and out. He was paid one pound a year.

The notes were probably made by the rector at a time when access to education in the village was limited mostly to Sunday schools.

Church Cottage

Next door to St Petrock's is Church Cottage, the history of which has been documented by present owners Mike and Jo Harrison.

Early History and Structure

Church Cottage is built on what appears to be the boundary wall of the south edge of the graveyard of St Petrock's Church in Parracombe. The building has been known variously over the years as 'Church House', 'Church Ale House', 'Churchtown', 'Barton Cottage' and 'Church Cottage'.

Originally, the church would not have had pews and, as well as a place of worship, it would have been used for town meetings and events. During the late medieval period, 15th and early 16th centuries, it became 'fashionable' for pews to be placed in churches which meant the nave could no longer be used for meetings and other purposes. This trend led to the building of church houses, like this one, which were used for meetings etc.

Typically, a church house had a spacious kitchen and ale house (brewery) downstairs, with a large meeting room upstairs. And Parracombe's is no exception. On this basis, we can estimate the building of Church Cottage dates to the late 15th century or early 16th century. This would concur with the age of the main beam in the downstairs lounge which, according to Dr Stuart Blaylock, probably dates from the 16th century. He believes this beam is probably the oldest internal feature of the original house to remain.

The brewery would have been situated in the smaller downstairs room to the west of the cottage. Many ale houses were closed or changed in usage during the time of Oliver Cromwell, as they were banned by the Puritans in approximately 1650. It wouldn't last. The Unfinished History of Parracombe and the Heddon Valley says on page 54, that ale was served in 1760 to mark the succession of George III - and that ale was probably brewed at Church Cottage.

At the time, there would have been a huge fireplace in the kitchen, which had one wall about eight ft in depth. Renovations carried out some 50 years ago revealed there was once a staircase leading from the kitchen, although the reason it was blocked off remains a mystery.

Upstairs was the main meeting room which would have been open to the rafters. According to Dr Stuart Blaylock, the trusses in the main part of the building look like they date from the 17th or 18th century as the 'cross' at the top of the trusses was typical of that period. An adjoining building was eventually added and at some stage one house became two.

The trusses in the neighbouring building also overlap at the top in a cross in the same manner, yet overall the manner of construction is far inferior to the main building, with the size and depth of footings, width and construction of the walls, quality and size of the wood used in the roof all markedly different to the main building. So it must assumed that this building, to the east of the main part of the house and slightly smaller in height and depth, was a barn built later and then converted into a habitable dwelling, with the trusses likely the result of builders mimicking the main building. No one knows when it became habitable, or when it became known as Church Cottage East.

Pictures reveal a large 'porch' on the front of the building which presumably served as a vestibule for both front doors to the two cottages. It is not known when this was removed.

Barton Cottage

Just as St Petrock's was known by various names, so was Church Cottage. For a period, from at least 1840 through to the First World War, the building was known as Barton Cottage(s). The first record of this is in the 1840 Tithe Map. Strangely, St Petrock's Church is not shown, but the main building including the 'barn' extension and the outbuilding are outlined and are labelled Barton.

Further evidence appears in the 1880 Ordnance Survey Map where the Church is shown as St Helen's Church, and Church Cottage is clearly called Barton. The front porch is clearly visible on this map.

In the census documents of 1841 to 1891, there is no reference to Barton or Barton Cottage. The only addresses listed are 'Court Place' and 'Churchtown'. Then, in the census documents of 1901 and 1911, there are two listings for Barton Cottage in each census. This is undoubtedly the building that is now known as Church Cottage, which was surely listed as 'Churchtown' in previous census.

A sole reference to Court Barton appears in Arthur Smyth's 'History of Parracombe' which was written in approximately 1876. In this book, he describes Court Barton as being a run-down farm with poor quality land stretching up to Barton Ridge, with the 'old farmhouse standing close to the churchyard'. As the only known house close to the churchyard, we can assume this to be Church Cottage. Smyth says the house is owned by the Dovells of 'Killiton' but is "occupied by a labourer". This fits with what we know from the 1871 census, when John Gibbs and Josiah Down (both agricultural labourers) lived at the two cottages.

(The lane that runs from Churchtown towards The Ark and then turns south towards Holworthy is called 'Barton Lane' on both the 1880 and 1904 Ordnance Survey maps.)

Despite our research, there's still much we don't know about the original layout of the two cottages. But there is documentary evidence about the ownership of the properties, as well as who lived there.

When the building was originally constructed as a Church House in or around 1500, the property was obviously owned by the Church.

The next clue about ownership doesn't appear until 1815. On 16th September of that year, there was a 'Public Vestry Meeting' where a unanimous vote approved a motion to 'repair the house now standing in Parracombe Churchyard'. As this is surely Church Cottage, the assumption is the Church still had ownership of the building at that time.

Sometime after this, ownership of the building passed to the Dovell family, but we can find no reference to a sale in any of the minutes of Vestry meetings of the time.

From paperwork linked to subsequent sales, we know who then owned Church Cottage, although it was tenants rather than owners mentioned here who were resident.

Owners

William & Eliza Dovell – from an unknown date to 1846

The 1840 Tithe map lists William Dovell as the owner of Church Cottage (shown as 'Barton' on the map) and surrounding land. The 1841 census shows William living at Killington ('Killaton') as a farmer with his wife Eliza, and three children Mary (35), James (30) and Susan (30). In 1838, William Dovell farmed 94 acres. He died in 1846 and was buried at St

Petrock's, with the gravestone giving his age as 73. His wife is also recalled on the stone in her full name of Elizabeth. She died in 1862 at the age of 84. The farm and land passed to their son James.

James & Matilda Dovell – 1846 to 1894

James Dovell was born in 1811. In 1851, he lived in Killington and is described as a farmer owning 250 acres. By 1871, this had grown to 360 acres. It is reasonable to assume this included the two Church Cottages and the adjacent fields, as Killington is quite nearby. James died in 1894, aged 83, and was also buried in the graveyard. It seems he left the farm (including Church Cottages and the fields nearby) to his only son Francis (Frank) Dovell. Frank was born in 1847 and married Sarah in the 1870s.

Frank & Sarah Dovell - 1894 to 1929

Sarah Dovell (nee Kent) was born in 1849 and died on 9th June 1929, fifteen months before her husband. She is buried in the graveyard at Christ Church. There is a reference to Sarah Dovell living at 'Court Barton' in 1910. Could this be what's now known as Court Place? Further mystery surrounds Sarah, who wrote a will dated 30th April 1923 bequeathing the cottages to her daughters Caroline and Susan. It is

St Petrocks and the wall of Church Cottage after the lightning strike of 1908.

not known why she left the land and cottages to her daughters rather than her husband, who outlived her. At this distance it's impossible to tell if there was a family rift. However, Caroline Dovell later donated the gate to the newly built village hall and dedicated this to her mother, but not to her father. A stone is inscribed as such dated 1932.

Caroline Lavinia Mary Snow Dovell - 1929 to 1956

Both spinsters, Caroline and her sister Susan Blackmore Dovell had lived together in 'The Bungalow' when it was newly built. It's now known as The Haven, next to Church Cottage. After Susan's death in 1940, an 'Assent' was granted on 25th June 1941 with regard to Church Cottage in favour of Caroline Dovell. However, she lived at The Bungalow for the rest of her life.

On 1st October 1953, the North Devon Water Board ran the mains distribution pipe over the field to the east of Church Cottage and a covenant was written that gave them access rights to maintain the main if necessary.

Caroline Dovell died on 15th March 1955 and is buried in the graveyard at Christ Church. On 16th July 1956, a conveyance was signed by which the cottages, as well as the fields to the east of the property, passed from Miss Agnes Smith and Mr Leslie William Kent Smith (the 'representatives' of Miss Dovell) to Mr James Louis Lindsay, at the time the Conservative MP for North Devon, and his wife Bronwen Mary Lindsay.

Agnes and Leslie Smith were the grandchildren of Caroline's uncle John Kent – the brother of Caroline's mother Sarah Kent. This makes Agnes and Leslie the cousins once removed of Caroline, and presumably her closest relatives on her death. Our assumption is that they were acting as executors of Caroline's Estate.

James & Bronwen Lindsay of Heddon Hall - 1956

As well as Church Cottage, Mr and Mrs Lindsay owned Heddon Hall where they lived in the 1950s and 1960s. An MP for just one Parliament, he lost the seat in 1959 to Jeremy Thorpe, who represented the Liberal party, by just 362 votes. James Lindsay died, in August 1997, aged 90 while Bronwen died in 2003. They had three sons and one daughter.

But their ownership of the cottages was fleeting. In 1956, the same year in which they had purchased the cottages, the Lindsays sold Church Cottage West to Miss Grace Rouse (see below) as an owner-occupier. At around this time, certainly before 1959, Church Cottage East was sold to Miss Rouse's sister, Mrs Irene Jones, also as an owner-occupier.

The conclusion is that the Lindsays only owned Church Cottage for a few months at most but retained the land to the north and east for longer.

Thanks to the various census taken every ten years from 1841 we know who the identity of the occupiers or tenants of the cottages during that time.

Tenants

Church Cottage West

John Lords 1841

John Lords (45) is listed in the 1841 census as living at Churchtown, along with Sophia Dovell (25) and Richard Wedow (14).

John & Lydia Leworthy 1851

The 1851 census lists John (33) and Lydia (29) Leworthy as living at 'Churchtown', with their two children Elizabeth (3) and John (1).

John, Lydia and Elizabeth were born in Challacombe, whereas baby John was born in Parracombe. This suggests the family moved to Churchtown in approximately 1849. John worked as a 'farmer of 21 acres'. This is not a big farm, but nevertheless it is perhaps surprising that a farmer of land lived at Church Cottage at all.

William & Sarah Widden 1861

The 1861 census shows William Widden (44) living at 'Churchtown' with his wife Sarah (52). William was a 'farmer of 40 acres'. They had a house servant called Agnes Leworthy, aged just 12.

Josiah & Mary Down 1871

In 1871, Josiah (23) and Mary Down (25) lived at 'Churchtown' with their son Josiah (1). Josiah worked as an agricultural labourer.

Edward & Eleanor Ridge 1881

The 1881 census showed Edward Ridge (56) worked as an agricultural labourer and lived at 'Churchtown' with his wife Eleanor (60).

The 1891 census lists just one family living at 'Churchtown' being the Gibbs family whom I believe occupied Church Cottage East.

Alfred & Mary Ann Sabbett 1901

In the 1901 census, Alfred Sabbett (28) is listed as living at 'Barton Cottage' with his wife Mary Ann (28) and their daughter Emma (2). Alfred was born in West Down and worked as a farm labourer. Mary Ann was born in Brendon. Emma had been born in West Down, so the family must have only recently moved to Barton Cottage.

Walter & Mary Carnock 1911

As listed in the 1911 census, Walter Carnock (44) and his wife Mary (56) lived at Barton Cottage. They had married 14 years previously, but had no children. Mary had been born in Parracombe, but Walter was from Bristol. He worked as an 'iron miner'.

William Davey - to late 1920's

Mr & Mrs William Davey had three children listed as attending the village school - Francis in 1920, Ivy May in 1923, and Ernest in 1928. The school records their address as Church Cottage. The family moved away in the late 1920s to Porlock to run a pub. They presumably lived at Church Cottage West before the Hawkes (see below).

One other record relating to this time is that of Mrs Down who had two children, Stanley & Evelyn, listed as attending the village school in 1924. The records show them living in 'Churchtown'. Could she be related to Josiah & Mary who lived there in 1871?

George & Martha Hawkes - Late 1920's to 1930's

According to Parracombe's history book, George, a former railway worker, and Martha Hawkes, once ran a sweet shop from Dunbar Cottage, in the centre of Parracombe. At some stage in the late 1920s, they moved to Church Cottage West and set up a sweet shop there too. They used to sell sweets out of the window on the west wall of the cottage. A photo that shows the damage caused to the church by the lightning strike back in 1908 also reveals there is no window on the west wall at the time, so this was added before or during the Hawkes' time there.

As Essex-born George was born in 1857 and Martha in 1846, they must have been about 70 and 80 years old when they moved to Church Cottage.

Earlier photos of the cottage show that this west facing window did not exist in the early 1900s, so the assumption is that George and Martha had the window installed for the specific purpose of selling sweets.

Mrs Loui Crocombe - Late 1940's to about 1956

Mrs Loui (perhaps short for Louise) Crocombe was living in Church Cottage West in the early 1950's. She had a daughter Violet who is listed as attending the village school in 1941.

In 1941, Loui and Violet were listed as living at Lorraine Cottage in central Parracombe, and then in 1945 at Rectory Cottage in Martinhoe. They must have moved to Church Cottage West after this date.

Miss Grace Rouse - 1956 to 1972

Miss Grace Winifred Dorothy Rouse, born in 1891, purchased Church Cottage West on 29th September 1956 from Mr & Mrs Lindsay.

At the same time, Miss Rouse also purchased a vegetable garden on the other side of the bridleway. This land passed to Mrs Jones when Miss Rouse died and then on to Mrs Jones' daughter Doreen Laming in 1977 when Mrs Jones died.

During her time at Church Cottage West, Grace ran a sweet shop on a Sunday from the west facing window, just as Mr Hawkes and Ms Crocombe had done before her.

On 30th November 1972, Miss Rouse died and she left Church Cottage West to her sister Irene Jones who lived next door. Grace is buried in Christ Church graveyard.

Occupiers / Tenants of Church Cottage East

Charles & Elizabeth Dovell 1841

Charles (40) and Elizabeth Dovell (40) are listed in the 1841 census as living at 'Churchtown' with their four children Charles (18), Louisa (13), Helen (8) and John (6). It seems one daughter, Harriet, was missing from the census records. Charles senior was born in Pilton, and Elizabeth was born in Brendon.

Charles & Charlotte Dovell 1851

Charles (30), the son of Charles and Elizabeth Dovell above, is listed in the 1851 census as living at 'Churchtown' with his wife Charlotte (30) and four children Mary (7), Ellen (5), Jessie (4) and John (1). An agricultural labourer, Charles was born in Martinhoe while Charlotte came from Thornbury, north of Bristol.

By 1851, Charles and Elizabeth Dovell (who had been living at Churchtown in 1841) are listed as living at Mannacott in Martinhoe and farming 73 acres. Perhaps they were bequeathed this land from the extended Dovell family, who farmed in and around Killington and also owned the cottages at Churchtown. Charles and Elizabeth were living with four children – Louisa (26), Harriet (24), Helen (18) and John (15).

Thomas & Helen Skinner 1861

The 1861 census lists Thomas Skinner (27) as living at 'Churchtown' with his wife Helen (26) and his three children Helen (4), Thomas (2) and Laura (1). Thomas was an 'Officer of the Inland Revenue'.

John & Agnes Gibbs 1871

By 1871 John Gibbs (48) was living at 'Churchtown' with his wife Agnes (47), together with their five children Ann (13), William (8), Grace (6), Thomas (4) and Frederick (1). John worked as an agricultural labourer and was born in Parracombe. Agnes had come from Challacombe.

The family had moved from Brakebrook where they had lived at the time of the 1851 census. Thomas died in 1873, aged just 6 years, and is buried in St Petrock's churchyard.

Thomas & Elizabeth Walter 1881

The 1881 census lists Thomas Walter (38) living at 'Churchtown' with his wife Elizabeth (38) and five children Theresa (19), William (8), John (6), George (4) and Sebina (1). Thomas was an agricultural labourer.

Thirty years later, Elizabeth Walter was living at the bottom of the hill, at Prisonford, as a widower. She'd had ten children in all.

In 1881 John & Agnes Gibbs, who'd lived at Church Cottage a decade earlier, and had are living in Parracombe Lane with their 11 year old son Frederick.

John & Agnes Gibbs c.1886 to 1906

By the time of the 1891 census, John & Agnes Gibbs were back living at 'Churchtown' with their now 21 year old son Frederick. Both Frederick and John worked as agricultural labourers. They also list a 9 year old 'lodger' called Susan Harris.

At the turn of the 20th century, John & Agnes aged 78 and 77 are still living there, but the census now calls their home 'Barton Cottage'. (Indeed, this is how the property is identified on the 1880 OS Map.) Both John & Agnes are described as 'Pawpers'. They had a lodger living with them called John Cornish, a 78 year old widower who had been born in Loxhore.

John and Agnes died in 1906 within a month of one another, aged 83 and 82. They are buried together in St Petrock's churchyard – next to Church Cottage. They outlived son Fred, who is also remembered in the graveyard, as he died in 1903 aged 34.

Sidney Madge 1911

The 1911 census shows Sidney Madge living at 'Barton Cottage'. Sidney was 40 years old and married with two surviving children, but he is listed as living alone. He worked as a farm labourer and gardener. He was born in Langridge, Crediton.

Thomas & Alice Tossell – late 1920's to 1954

In the 1901 census, Thomas (30) & Elizabeth Tossell (27) are listed as living at 'Church Lane'. In the 1911 census, they are listed as living at 'Churchtown'. Thomas & Elizabeth had several children - Henry, Charley, William, Thomas & Lily. Thomas junior shows on the 1911 census as living with his parents at 'Churchtown' aged 7. In 1901 and 1911, Church Cottage is listed as 'Barton Cottage' so the Tossell family did not live there at this time.

Thomas junior married Alice and, at some stage, moved into Church Cottage East – living there through to 1954, when they moved to one of the new council houses that had been built at Ash Park in Bodley Lane, Parracombe. They are listed in the 1931 census as being at Church Cottage. Thomas junior was a manual worker working in the quarry in 1931, whilst Alice did house work for other families.

Thomas senior died on 23rd May 1948, and Elizabeth died on 28th June 1952.

Fred & Christine Sanders - 1954 to 1956

When Fred and Christine Sanders lived at Brakebrook there was a serious fire and, as a result, they moved into Church Cottage East after Thomas & Alice Tossell had moved to Ash Park. When the cottage was sold to Irene Jones (presumed 1956), it is not known where the Sanders moved to.

Mrs Irene Jones - Mid 1950's to 1977

Irene Jones, born in 1898, was the younger sister of Grace Rouse. It is not known when Irene purchased Church Cottage East or who from. The best guess is that it was at about the same time as her sister Grace purchased Church Cottage East (1956), and it is reasonable to assume the purchase was also from Mr & Mrs James Lindsay, who had purchased the land and cottages in 1956 from the estate of Caroline Dovell.

On 9th October 1959, before any listing of the property, Irene Jones applied for, and gained permission to extend the property to the east. This involved demolishing the small larder and replacing it with a much larger single storey flat-roof structure which, according to the plans, would house a small larder, a bathroom, a separate toilet, and an immersion heater for the hot water. The plans also showed the routing of the sewer connections to the mains drains to the front of the property.

Irene Jones was the cook at the village school and she is remembered as being 'very strict'. Irene was not originally from North Devon – it seems she came from Surbiton and moved to Parracombe after she separated from her husband. The exact circumstances, and whether her sister Grace came before, or after, or with Irene, are not known; but the fact that her daughter Doreen was living in Surbiton at the time of Irene's death in 1977 ties in. Anecdotally, the family name Rouse is historically quite common in the Parracombe area.

Irene Jones (nee Rouse) died on 7th December 1977 and is buried in Christ Church graveyard.

Owner Occupiers of Church Cottage as 'One House'

From 1972, when Grace Rouse died, both properties were owned by Irene Jones. At some stage between 1972 and 1977, before Irene died, a door was created at ground floor level to connect the two properties. In addition, the front door to Church Cottage West was blocked. At first floor level, the two properties remained separate with no connecting passageway.

We know the above because this was how the house was when Richard & Philippa Wainwright purchased the house from Doreen Betty Laming, the surviving daughter and heir of Irene Jones who, on the date of the sale, was recorded as living in Surbiton, Surrey.

Graveyard Tales

Under this marble reduced to ashes will fatten the body Johannis Newell former rector of the church who departed this life 5th day of February 1681 aged 70 which will always be painful. (Translation)

St Petrock's is one of the most atmospheric, undiscovered jewels of Exmoor. If you haven't been before, there's a treat in store both within the walls of this ancient church and outside. Take time to explore its charm.

This section is about the men, women and children buried in the church and graveyard. According to the 1840 Tithe Map, the churchyard at the time measured one rood and 34 perches, almost half an acre. Today, there are upwards of 130 graves, containing the remains of hundreds of people.

This is by no means a definitive history, but we've put as much as we can say with certainty against the tombstones arrayed here. The inscriptions below are, for the moment, taken from two books published more than 100 years ago with additional information from newspaper reports and diaries of the time.

Despite having those birth, marriage and death records for assorted eras, it's still difficult to approach this section with clarity. It starts with stories about which we have specific information.

After that, there seem to be numerous repetitions, with the same person mentioned on several headstones. Or are these the names of two different people altogether?

Without additional forensic research, it's impossible to tell if two people who share a surname are brothers or sons, aunts or mothers – or even one and the same person appearing in different documents.

It doesn't help that the name of infants who died young were used for subsequent children – who sometimes themselves also suffered an untimely death. For example, Richard and Eleanor Nicholls had a son, Philip, in 1756 and another of the same name four years later in 1760.

There's confusion too, caused by names as well as dates. It turns out Richord was a girl's name – as was Isaat, Ilett and Izett. One surname appears as 'fflamanck' (John, born to John and Frances in 1756). Other names evolve with a variety of spellings, with letters added or taken away within a few short years.

They also tell the stories of family heartache caused by a volley of infant deaths, which might have been caused by cholera, tuberculosis, typhoid and other diseases which have since been consigned to history.

Weather is taking its toll on the condition of the stones. In addition, an unknown number of graves and headstones have been lost in time. According to the 1917 register produced by the Devon and Cornwall Record Society, the earliest records for burials go back to 1687. One must assume there were many more prior to that and visitors would struggle to find any 17th century graves in the churchyard today. Burials continued at St Petrock's even after the opening of Christ Church and conversely, there are some comparatively recent additions. There's a headstone for Florence Henriette Crocombe, who died in 1969, that also remembers her sisters Emily Kate and Clara Blanche, who were both cremated elsewhere. William and Lavinia Lang were buried there in 1952 and 1966 respectively, with a headstone that reads 'Resting where no shadows fall.' It's unclear if the underlining of the word has significance.

It seems the final additions to the graveyard were in 1979 when Ethel Beatrice Stenner Blackmore, spinster and schoolmistress, died, followed by sister Christine in 1986.

By charting the gravestones, we've often come up with more questions than answers. For most people information like this presents a maze that's confusing, even chaotic, with various inscriptions luring the unwary down ancestral dead ends. Those who an inclination towards making family trees will probably have a different view. But even those with the greatest enthusiasm for genealogy will find St Petrock's graveyard a challenge. Where there's been an absence of evidence, we've done the minimum of cross-referencing.

Despite the confusions caused, some of the indisputable facts from the church register might resolve outstanding issues for some genealogists. We've divided this inscriptions into two sections here: inside and outside the church.

Inside the Church

One of the graves in the floor of the church belongs to John Newell. Also known as Johannis, a Latin version of John, he was a vicar at St Petrock's who died in 1682. His will, kept in the National Archives, surely reveals he was uncommonly wealthy for the time.

The inventory of his 'goods and chattels' was drawn up by Thomas Lewardlewe and Matthew Holy on 5 April 1682 and went like this:

All his wearing apparel rings, gold and money in his purse £230
His Bachelor of Divinity hood 10 s
His debts due upon speciality £510
His debts due upon speciality but deceipts (?) £306
The rents and money due without speciality £100
The lands and chattels not conveyed £2,810
All his plate and one was £12 12s
All his bedsteads and bedding £74 8s
All his table boards, settles, forms and two pestles and mortars £4 2s
All his martial arms £2
All his ampules, scriptores, counters, chests, boxes, trunks, coffers, close stool, malt hutch and [illegible] stuff £9 10s
All his reives, trendells, corbutts, pales, hogsheads and all other timber vessels £2 13s
One hewing stock, two pair of sickles and a pair of bellows, three flasks and all his baskets, one jack, one clock and all his bottles and glasses £5 10s
All his candles, tallow and [illegible] 15s
All his syrup, sugar and other confectionery, china clomb and all other commodities in his closet 10s
All his library £150
His periwig £1
His looking glasses 10s

All his carpets, cushions, chairs, stools and their coverings £10
All his tables clothes, cupboard clothes, tablenapkins and all other his table linen 6d
All his wool £4
All his bags, leeps, cazzons, sives, rangers and peckes 10s
All his trenchers, earthernware, the dining lumber £1 10s
All his brass, pewter and latten £23 15s
All his iron implements £2 15s 9d
All his cows, calves and other bullocks £300
All his sheep £10
All his nags and mares £18
All his pigs £3 10s
All his poultry £1 10s
All his corn and grain growing, threshed in barns and mown £12 10s
All his malt £3 10s
All his hackney saddles, bridles, pillions, riding clothes and pack saddles with their appurtenances £1 10s
All his rope halters, harness and tresses [illegible] cart wheels, drawers, harness crocks, dung botts and all his other house implements 10s
All his shovels, maddocks, picks, barrows, handbarrows, wheelbarrows, hooke [illegible], pinsers, endscrapes, rakes, weeding [illegible] gaffs and all other his implements for husbandry £1
All his hay, straw and fodder £1
All his turfs, woods and fuel £1
All his pig troughs 4s
All the rest of the goods omitted and forgotten 16s

Total £4,468 4 s 4 d

Some items included in the list have different names today. Ammpules, are likely vessels for storing wine while a jack was a leather bottle. Cazzons was the name for dried cattle dung used for fuel, a peck the raw skin of a sheep while latten was a type of brass. A trendal was a hoop to which candles were fixed. However, interpreting the meaning of clomb, leeps, rangers, peckes and endscrapes has proved more challenging. That Newell bequeathed a clock in his will is an indication of his considerable wealth.

Newell was also the incumbent at Combe Martin church and he was there when he died, as the town's church register reveals: '1681. The 4th day of Feb: died Mr Newell, minister of this parish, and was buried at Parracombe ye Thursday after'.

Then there's a series of monuments that amply illustrate the difficulties in untangling families that favoured using the same Christian name. On the south wall, there's a marbled wood wall tablet, some 1.8 metres high and 1.15 metres wide, embellished with two wooden urns. It's dedicated to Walter Lock (17/9/1667), Walter Lock (7/7/1732), David Lock – son of Walter Lock (3/2/1742) and Rebecca Lock, wife of David (29/9/1770).

Another, slightly taller and wider and likewise decorated with urns, is dedicated to David Lock, who died in 1786, his sister Joan Roach (1762-1837) and her son Richard Roach, who was eight when he died in 1797. Another son, also called Richard after he was born in 1799, pre-deceased her, aged 19.

Finally, a third tablet appears to echo the sentiments for Joan, her husband Richard Roach, who died in 1817, and John Lock, another of Joan's brothers who died in 1803.

Putting Flesh on the Bones

(Monument dedications according to the 1917 book are in plain type while explanations are in italic.)

(Brick altar tomb). John Gammin, died 14 July 1854, aged 21. John Gammin, father of above, died 15 September 1859, aged 51. Maria Gammin, wife of above, died 31 March 1861, aged 53, Susanna Blackmore, mother of above John Gammin senior, died 2 November 1865, aged 81. Emma, wife of Richard Gammin of Rowley, died 3 August 1882, aged 38. Richard Gammin, above named, died 13 March 1889, aged 48. Agnes Sloley, daughter of above Richard and Emma Gammin, died 23 December 1893, aged 24. Bessie Gammin, daughter of above Richard & Emma Gammin, died 31 January 1914, aged 35.

Farmer and keen cricketer Richard Gammin died in 1889 after throwing himself in Pinkery Pond. He was despondent, having been unlucky in love. When it was revealed, the story of his demise transfixed the neighbourhood.

Years before the tragedy Richard had married to farmer's daughter Emma Gill while his older brother Joseph wed her younger sister Ann. These young wives were from a Braunton family. In 1876 Richard had been admired as a farmer by reporter Arthur Smyth who described him as 'an energetic young farmer with plenty of practical experience. His motto seems to be "improvement and high farming" for he has done wonders to the place Rowley Down'.

Within a dozen years Richard's fortunes had dramatically changed. A widower for six years, with wife Emma dying seven years earlier aged 38, he was a lonely father of ten and it seems he despaired after attempts to woo a Parracombe woman were rebuffed. Her letter, refusing his advances, was found in his jacket found folded at the water's edge. But while that neat and lonely pile of clothes made it clear he wanted to end his life, of his body there was no sign. Lynmouth life boat was dispatched to the site to find Richard's body, as well as a diver from Wales. When they failed it was decided to drain the pond - but the bungs that kept the water in the man-made lake wouldn't budge. In the end Bob Jones, who built the Lynton-Lynmouth Cliff Railway, devised a ram to shift the stubborn bungs and Gammin's remains were revealed. About 1,000 people turned up to watch the grisly spectacle and postcards were made of the event.

A wealthy farmer owning some 756 acres surrounding his home at Rowley Barton and three labourers in his employ, Richard left estate valued at £1,800 – worth some £233,000 today.

Richard was buried, after the closure of St Petrock's, in the altar tomb with other members of his family, including his oldest brother John who died in 1854. Daughters Agnes and Bessie are mentioned in the inscription. His other children were Emma, Annie, John William, Frederick, Henry, Mary and George. Mysteriously, George – who moved to the Midlands as a young man to work as an ironmonger - appears in the 1891 census to have been born after Emma's death. This is likely to be a date anomaly.

The Gammin family had lived in Parracombe for

generations. In 1806, his grandfather, John Gammin, married Susanna Slader, described in the register as a minor. The union happened with the consent of her guardian, Rev John Blackmore of Charles. By 1812, Susanna, already a widow, married John Blackmore, who had also lost his wife. That's why her surname differs from the rest. But she had a son, John, from her first marriage.

He duly married and became a father and, with son John 'Gammin' is registered as Gammon in July 1833, two years before a sister, Mary, appeared. At the time the family lived at Highley. Brother Joseph was born in 1838, three years before the ill-fated Richard, and sister Ann three years afterwards, in 1844.

Richard's father, John Gammin, died suddenly in a field at Tucking Mill in 1859, on his way to Highley. An inquest was held the day after he died which found a ruptured blood vessel was the cause of death.

John Tamlyn, son of James and Mary Tamlyn of this parish, died 18 February 1847, aged 14 weeks.

Grace Tamlyn, daughter of James Tamlyn deceased and Mary, his wife, of this parish died 3 August 1846, aged 20.

James Tamlyn of this parish died 28 January 1841 aged 58. Mary Tamlyn, widow of above James Tamlyn died 17 September 1859 aged 73.

Another story of suicide is revealed on a headstone dedicated to the Tamlyn family. The Tamlyns likely moved to Parracombe after marrying elsewhere and had at least five children. William was born in 1819, when his father was listed as a farmer at West Hill. Susannah was born in 1821, John in 1824, Grace in 1825 and Henry in 1827.

The death of Henry Tamlyn, aged one day, is recorded in 1827. Tragic though this must have been, it is Grace who garners our attention for her sad story. Thanks to a diary entry by William Watts in the summer of 1846, it's clear that she committed suicide at a time when that was taboo - although a law passed in 1823 meant victims could be buried in a Christian manner. (Previously the bodies of those who took their own lives were not permitted to be buried in consecrated ground, usually being committed to graves at busy intersections.)

While it was undoubtedly a subject shrouded in shame, it seems people in Parracombe trod their own path in this case. According to Watts' diary: 'A hearse passed here with the body of Grace Tamblyn [sic], a young woman who cut her throat with a razor at Charles and died immediately . . . Buried in Parracombe Church by the Reverend J Dovell who had the service from the church gate direct to the grave but at the earnest wish of friends she was carried into the church.'

The circumstances of her death are shocking and today no one knows why she committed suicide. Extreme poverty, mental illness and unplanned pregnancies were likely causes during the era. Grace's headstone cost one pound and 12 shillings. Church records show she had been baptised at St Petrock's on 16th October 1825.

After discussing Grace's burial, Watts reveals: 'A child of John and Maria Hill was buried at the same time without service, it not having been baptised.'

At the time – and for decades afterwards - still-born or infants who hadn't been christened were buried in the same casket with others recently dead, and that seems to have been what happened here. It wasn't John and Maria's only child. When Maria Hill died in 184,8 she left five motherless children – and her husband married again within six months (see p 34).

As for the Tamlyns, James and Mary were already living at West Hill when son John was born in 1824. John grew up and married Margaret Blackmore in 1849, with the couple naming their first daughter, born the year they were wed, Grace in a touching tribute to John's sister. However, the child only lived for three years. Another daughter, born in 1854 was also named Grace and she survived into the 20th century. She had brothers

John, James and William and sisters Susan, Mary and Elizabeth, who was born when Margaret was 47. John died in 1881 while his wife passed away in 1909.

According to his diary, it was Watts who had put up the gravestone in memory of James Tamlyn, on 24 June 1841, some six months after his death. Afterwards William Watts' daughter Maria went to live with Mrs Tamlyn at West Hill aged 12, presumably as a maid.

Grace Barwick, wife of Thomas Barwick of this parish, died 16 January 1850 aged 76. Thomas Barwick, above named, died 7 December 1855 aged 80.

[It's Thomas 'May' Barwick, according to the Parish Register.)

Thomas May Barwick, a carpenter, married Grace Squire on 6 October 1800.

The baptism of Thomas and Grace's daughter Mary is recorded on 17 July 1803. Three years later, daughter Ann is baptised on 11 March 1806, Susanna on 3 July 1808, Johanna on 4 April 1811, Elizabeth, 2 August 1813, and Nathaniel, 22 April 1816 – when Thomas is described as a carpenter and the family are placed in Prisonford. One Joannna Barwic, of Prisonford, died aged 65 in 1815, possibly a relative of Thomas'. But if diarist William Watts is to be believed, this may not have been one big happy family.

One can only speculate on her character and the circumstances in which she died but Watts remarks about Grace's passing in his notes, declaring: 'the end of the wicked is miserable'.

Clearly the hatchet had been buried by the time Thomas died as William was a bearer at his funeral, with William Blackmore, Nath Sloley and William Burden.

Noah Palmer, died 23 May 1884. [According to Parish Register 27 March 1884 aged 75, although that gives us a slight discrepancy with his age.]

Maria Palmer, wife of above, died 12 May 1903 aged 90.

Noah Palmer was the illegitimate son of Elizabeth Palmer, baptised on 28 January 1807. He married Maria Richards on 25 March 1834. Maria and Noah had a daughter, Eliza, in 1835 when they were recorded as living at Rowley. The following year, they were living in Bodley when daughter Helen arrived. However, it's generally accepted that he built or lived in a house on land above the church and today's A39. In the 1851 census, he was recorded as living in Ladyswell Cottage, Mount Pleasant, but it was quickly dubbed 'Noah's Ark'.

Eliza and Helen were followed by brothers William, John, Noah and James. According to William Watts, Noah Palmer had another child buried at St Petrock's on 30 November 1846 'and in the evening Charles Blackmore buried his child in his garden'.

In the 1850 White's Directory, Noah Palmer is recorded as the parish clerk and within six years he had added 'letter carrier' as his occupation. But subsequent census entries reveal he and Maria moved from Ladyswell Cottage into the village and he was working as an agricultural labourer, even in his seventies.

Clearly, there was a great deal of affection for Noah and his wife in the village. Rev Peter Nettleton Leakey, who presided over the building of the new church, at one stage wrote to the North Devon Journal appealing for help for the family.

'Noah Palmer, a highly respected man of this parish in the 70th year of his age, has lately broken down in his work as postman in which capacity for nearly 18 years he has delivered letters in this district, walking daily over 10 miles in very rough and hilly country. He is not entitled to a pension as he received only eight shillings and, for some time, six shillings a week. He can do but little for himself and a sick wife. He is a truly Godly man and for over 30 years has acted as parish clerk in this parish. It is now proposed to purchase for him a

small annuity.'

Sophia, wife of George Smyth, born 17 October 1812, died 24 March 1883. Also George Smyth, born 3 January 1811, died 15 May 1900.

George Smyth was in fact a Wesleyan, who built the chapel opposite the Fox & Goose pub in 1839. According to one relative, George liked to dress in billowing trousers and would offer a boot rather than a hand when he met people. A noted philanthropist, he gave away 'tickets' for meat and coal to poorer residents in the village. He also kept the only grapevine in the village. His wife Sophia was the youngest of ten Blackmore children. Her great nephew Henry wrote of the kindness of both, recalling how there were teas at the Wesleyan Chapel for the poor, with free tickets for meal, coal and other necessities being dished out by the Smyths. Sophia was, he said, 'the grandest cook in the neighbourhood. She used to come up and help mother at pay days and other great festivals. In all cases of sickness she was the Samaritan of the parish'. A monument to George Huxtable Smyth, who died in 1848 aged three after an attack of croup, was put in the chapel by parents George and Sophia. Arthur Smyth, who became a village correspondent, was another of their sons. Given the historic rivalry between the churches, felt in Parracombe and elsewhere, George and Sophia probably ended up in a grave at St Petrock's because the church had already closed.

In loving memory of a dear husband and father William Leworthy who lost his life in the flood August 15th 1952

On 15 August 1952, rainwater, that had accumulated behind the block drainage holes of a disused railway culvert, burst through, sweeping down the River Heddon and picking up boulders and trees in its path. Postman William Leworthy was killed as he braved the terrible weather to check up on the welfare of his sister. He'd spent the afternoon helping a farmer at West Bodley with the corn. That night thirty-two men, women and children around the region died and 92 homes were destroyed. Family friend Gilbert Walters left a description of that night, recalling that William John Leworthy lived at Rose Cottage with wife Mabel Jane and sons Derek Samuel and Montague William John. He was a trapper in the winter and an odd job man in the summer.

'On the afternoon of Friday, 15 August the weather had been atrocious and during the evening it never ceased to rain. Late in the evening William decided to go out into the village to see what damage had been done. His sister lived at Chippy's Cottage, now known as Half Pint, and in those days it was

Lynmouth's flood also claimed a victim in Parracombe

often flooded.

'He went out on his own and took a Tilley lamp. Just before 10 pm, the embankment above the village was washed away causing a tidal wave to come through the village, the water being six ft high. Later his Tilley lamp was found, and the following morning, his body was found at Skilley Bridge. My father was one of those that went out to bring him home.'

After her death in 1959, Mabel was buried in the same grave.

(Altar tomb)

Underneath are the remains of two sons and daughters of William Roach & Molly, his wife, of this parish. Mary, died 19 September (?1797)in the- - years of her age. William, died 16 February - - - - -, Maria, died - - - aged 14 years, Richard, died I July - - - , Molly, wife of William Roach, abovenamed, died 15 October (?1825) aged (?31) years - - - William Roach - - - - (all this stone is much worn and very difficult to decipher.)

William and Molly had a son, also called William, in 1791. In 1803, Richard Roach was born to William and Mary. But it seems tragedy befell the family, which lived at 'Paracomb Mill'. William Roach died in February 1814, aged 22. Maria Roach died there in June aged 14 while Richard Roach perished a month later aged 11. Although there was widespread hunger at the time caused by the Napoleonic Wars, it seems likely they fell victim to disease. (The deaths of Mary and Richard Roach are both recorded in 1797 but there's no indication of their ages or relationship.) William's death is recorded in December 1824, when he was aged 63, a year after Molly died at Parracombe Mill, aged 54.

Here lies the body of Mary, wife of John Slader of the - - - - - died (?7) April 1779.

Here lies the body of John Slader the elder of this parish, who died 6 February 1789, in his 75th year.

In August 1736, three sisters gave birth in the vicinity of St Petrock's, including Mary Slader who was married to John and gave their son the same name. Other sisters were Richord Marchant who gave birth to a daughter, also called Richord, with husband Anthony, and Joan Harton, who had a daughter Elizabeth with husband Richard. All were the daughters of John and Margaret Lord of 'Chalacomb Rawley'. The records indicate that Mary and sister Richord both died in the same year.

Here lies the body of Richord Marchant relict of Anthony Marchant of this parish, she died 10 January 17 - - in the 76th year of her age.

Anthony and Richord lost three daughters named Mary. The first two died within weeks of being born in 1734 and 1735. The third died in 1750, aged five. There were other children, however; daughter Elizabeth in 1733, daughter Richord in 1736, son Humphry in 1738 and daughter Susanna in 1741. Richord married Phillip Tooker in 1754. The year of mother Richord's death was 1779, some eight years after her husband's.

Thomas Walters died 13 February 1907 aged 65.

Thomas had been born in North Petherton while wife Elizabeth came from Combe Martin. He was the father of Frederick Edward Walters who died in the First World War, aged 35, who is also recalled on the gravestone. When he died Frederick was a sergeant in the Australian infantry, having previously emigrated to become a timber worker. Records show he had a union flag tattooed on his forearm. Signing up soon after the war broke out, Frederick served in Gallipoli where he received gunshot wounds. After his recovery he was shipped to France in time for the Battle of the Somme. During the heat of one day's fighting he was twice promoted. He died within three weeks of arriving. Sgt Walters was the youngest of ten children, his siblings being Lucy, Thirza, Sabrina, Mary, Bessie, Thomas, William, John and George. This large family lived at

Prisonford.

(Large enclosure with altar tomb within high front railings). On E side George Pyke, 2nd son of Rev John Pyke and Elizabeth his wife b 5 November 1843, died 13 May 1859. Marianne Nott, his aunt, born 1807, died 1880. On N side, Elizabeth Pyke, daughter of John Nott Esq of Bydown House, Swimbridge and wife of Rev John Pyke, rector of this parish b 19 September 1807, died 13 March 1858. Rev John Pyke M A J P Patron and 42 years rector of this parish, b 29 December 1798, died 25 January 1868. Adrian Stephen Pyke Nott, his grandson, on 15th d 20 April 1882. On W side, coat of arms. On S side James Nott Pyke Esq b 22 February 1815, died 30 August 1859.

William Watts described 16 year old George Pyke's funeral, to which he had been invited: 'Had hat band and white kid gloves. I walked next to Rev C Scriven and Dr Clarke with Mr Wills of Barnstaple and the bearers were Joseph Gammin and Rev Gammin, John Smyth and James Smyth, John Blackmore and Charles Blackmore, William Somerville and Lewis Somerville. Rev Mr Pyke walked with the Rev Mr Arther and then came Rev Mr Nott, Mr Snow, Mr Burden and Mr Dovel etc and the servants etc'

William Watts was clearly on good terms with Rev Pyke. On Christmas Day 1841, he says: 'We all invited to dinner and tea at the Reverend Mr Pyke's. I and May, William and Philip went and the children had 6d each given them by Mr Pyke. Maria and baby was ill and did not go'. It was the first of many Christmases spent together and it was Rev Pyke who christened the baby, Martha, in February.

It was a relative, John Pyke Nott, of Bydown House, Swimbridge, who donated the freehold of the present school, on 29 December 1881, amounting to 18 perches of land.

However, there was an absence of affection when it came to Pyke's two sons, John and James, also Oxford graduates. He called them 'overbearing' and accused them of killing sheep dogs and cats which they said disturbed the game on their land: 'They wanted to shoot over every person's land but would allow no one to shoot over theirs. As scarcely anyone ever went shooting nothing much was said until their dogs or cats disappeared, and then there was a rumpus. But as nothing could be proved it was like two puppies – all growl without any biting'. It was James who later left a bequest to St Petrock's.

Four sons of Robert and Susanna Ralph of this parish. Fred died 27 February 1870 aged 14 days, Frederick died 22 October 1874, aged three years, Henry died 15 April 1880, aged six months. William, died 5 March 1885 in the 19th year of his age.

Another story of heartbreak revealed by the gravestones. William was a farm servant at the Crocombe's farm at Holworthy at the time. There's an account of William's death in a letter sent by 12 year old Reuben Blackmore from his home, Court Place, on 27 April 1885, to his brother Henry living in London. 'It was a very sad thing about William Ralph,' he wrote. 'He was in his usual state of health when he got up and as he was cleaning down his horse John Bray heard a rattle in his throat and he fell against his horse and dropt [sic] down dead. John Bray then called Miss Bessie Crocombe and they carried him in the house. He was buried on the following Monday, there were more people then than there has been for some times, and thirty forester.' There's no further sign of the Ralphs in the records that we have so perhaps the family line died with William.

Emma, wife of Charles Blackmore, died 30 May 1886, aged 44. The above named Charles Blackmore, died 30 November 1900, aged 59.

Emma is described by son Henry as the 'ideal mother and a real Christian. Every morning before starting her work she would read a chapter from the Bible then lift each one of us individually to our heavenly father in prayer'. His writings under the title 'The Story of a Unit' recall how he was labelled a dunce at school and bear all the hallmarks of someone suffering dyslexia. His inability to grasp reading and writing at the same speed as his siblings had not gone unnoticed by his mother. She would write to him twice weekly but, he reveals, just two months before her death, when he was living in London, she returned one of his letters apparently unread on account of its poor handwriting and inadequate composition. Henry was by her side when she died in May 1886 and reveals: 'I found out the reason for all these letters which was a mother's love for her children, for she told me I was a weakling and my business and future laid [sic] very near her heart.' When he told her that his painting job in London was going well 'it pleased her very much'.

(Altar tomb) In memory of Eleanore Blackmore, wife of John Blackmore of Court Place in this parish, died 19 December 1831, aged 45, buried in the adjoining grave on the S side of this vault. Underneath, in this vault are the remains of Richard Blackmore (to whose memory this tomb was erected), the son of John Blackmore and Eleanor, his wife aforementioned. He died 24 December 1845, aged 32.

Eleanor and John married at St Petrock's Church on 16 September 1811, some four months before eldest son John was baptised there. At least three of Eleanor's children headed for America – John, Eliza and Walter. Years later, the family heard that John left a fortune worth several hundred thousand dollars after his death in America, shortly before the turn of the 20th century.

In memory of Mary Ann, wife of John Blackmore before named, died 21 November 1858, aged 58. In memory of John Blackmore died 31 August 1869, aged 78. Rosa Cullam, died 18 March 1877, aged 26. Oscar Richard Blackmore, son of Charles and Emma Blackmore, died 18 October 1882, aged 11 weeks. (Oscar had a twin brother called William.) Emma, wife of Charles Blackmore, died 30 May 1886, aged 44. On slab on E side - All scaled off except 'Blackmore'. On N side, Elizabeth Blackmore, relict of John Blackmore of this parish, died 29 September 1821 in the 83rd year of her age. On S side Epitaph only. On W side, John Blackmore of this parish, died 30 March 1805 in the 66th year of his age.

Mary Ann was John Blackmore's second wife

Here lies the body of Dorothy Burgess, of this parish of Challacombe, d -- July 1753, aged 52.

Richard Blackmore of this parish, died 15 May 1842, aged 75. Elizabeth Blackmore, wife of the above, died 14 August 1832, aged 64.

After marrying in 1789, Richard and Elizabeth lived at Court Farm, which they built in 1791. Six of their ten children married and between them produced 41 grandchildren. While eldest son John eventually took on the farm, two sons – Richard and William – with their wives and families emigrated to North America. Richard is thought to have left about 1832, with his wife Philippa, originally from Torrington, travelled in the barque Calypso the following year with their six children. Some of John's children - John, Eliza and Walter – also emigrated, with one family story holding that Walter died at sea. In 1850, William, wife Charity, her unmarried sister Mary Gould and six children between them headed for Quebec. Later they were joined by other members of the family.

One son and two daughters of Edwin & Sylvia Antell, Lily Grace died 27 July 1886 aged 3 years. Charles died 27 January 1896 aged five months. Minnie Eliza died 20 November 1905 aged 14 years. Alfred John Pearce Antell son of above died 15 September 1912 aged 26.

Stoker Edwin James Antell, another son of Edwin and Sylvia of Headnacott, died aged 40 when HMS

Goliath was torpedoed in the Mediterranean. His ship was lost on 13 May 1915 as it took part in the Gallipoli campaign, with Britain trying and failing to knock Turkey out of the First World War. Edwin had been a servant to William Lock of East Bodley before joining the Royal Navy in 1898. Two days later his brother Fred also signed up. After more than a decade in service, he was leading stoker when he finally left in 1909. However, at the outbreak of the First World War he was recalled, leaving wife Annie and his infant son, also called Edwin. He is remembered on the Plymouth War Memorial and also at Christ Church. According to family sources, Fred's wife Mabel was hanging out washing when she received a telegram saying her husband had been killed in action. The shock turned her hair white overnight and it was some time before she discovered it was in fact his brother who was dead. Fred returned in 1919 to resume his job as postman. Their mother Sylvia was a victim of the Spanish flu epidemic in 1918.

Reuben George Berry died 23 July 1889 aged 4 years and 8 months. Herbert Ernest Berry died 24 July 1889 aged six years and eight months. Ledford Blanche Berry died 8 August 1889 aged 1 year and 3 months. Thomas Berry died 20 March 1909 aged 64 years.

The Berrys, who lived at Voley, were badly scarred, possibly by a bout of diptheria. Happily, other children followed but there was more misery in store for mother Martha, even after the death of husband Thomas. Another son, Ira Sydney Berry, known as Ted, who once worked as a plate layer on the railway, joined the Royal Navy after the outbreak of the First World War. He became a marine gunner on HMS Good Hope, which sank with all hands on 1 November 1914 in the Battle of Coronel, off Chile after a British flotilla was outgunned by the German navy. His name doesn't appear on the Parracombe war memorial. At the time of his death, mother Martha was living in Swansea and that's where he is remembered, as well as the Portsmouth war memorial.

The Dovells

There are a collection of memorials to the Dovell family, whose fortunes were intertwined with the Blackmores, among others.

In memory of Peter Dovell, son of William & Elizabeth, his wife, died at Columbia, Brazoria County, Texas, 24 December 1840, aged 27. Also in this vault are deposited the remains of William Dovell, afore named, died 12 January 1846, aged 73. On S side, Mary Dovell, daughter of William Dovell, died 12 March 1848, aged 44. Elizabeth Dovell, relict of William Dovell, died 3 April 1862, aged 84.

(Altar tomb) Underneath are the remains of Richard Dovell who died 11 May 1793 in the 83rd year of his age. Also the remains of William Dovell who died 12 July 1793 in the 85th year of his age, both of West Middleton in this parish. Also the remains of William Dovell, grandson of the above-named William Dovell and eldest son of the late William and Jane Dovell of West Middleton in this parish, he died 11 December 1846 in the 66th year of his age. Also the remains of Rebecca Dovell, wife of Philip Dovell of East Middleton. She died on 14 December 1848 aged 76. Also the remains of Rev Joseph Dovell, rector of Martinhoe and the youngest son of William and Jane Dovell of West Middleton in this parish before named. He died 25 December 1856 in the 57th year of his age. Also the remains of Philip Dovell of East Middleton (son of William and Jane Dovell) of West Middleton who died 4 May 1864 aged 73. On S side, headstone attached sideways - Here lies the body of Philip Dovell of this parish who died 9 May 1753 in the 79th year of his age. Also in memory of William Dovell and Richard Dovell, of this parish, joint executor of the above, died 11 May 1793 in the 85th year of his age.

In his diary, William Watts records that William Dovell died in Barnstaple and describes how the body was returned to Parracombe. 'A hearse and two carriages came here from Barnstaple with the body of Mr W Dovell, about 20 on horseback all with long silk hat bands and the eight bearers wore cloaks.'

In October 1847, Watts put up the 'excellent' headstone dedicated to William Dovell, which was also dedicated to the dead man's grandfather, William Dovell, and his grandfather's brother Richard. The costs was two pounds three shillings and ten pence.

It is possibly that another gravestone was put up in memory of William as Watts records one in 1847, to William Dovell, of Killington, who was the brother of the late Reverend and Mrs Dovell of Martinhoe. The cost this time was one pound and nine shillings.

There's one outstanding story about a Dovell recalled by Arthur Smyth. He once related a story about a Captain Dovell who, he maintains, was born at Killington and buried at St Petrock's.

'He hated farming, and at last his family gave him his desire and he went to sea. At last, as captain of an East Indiaman (his own), he took his wife and son, a boy of eight years, with him to sea. The vessel was wrecked. He never saw the boy, but he caught his wife and swam for hours; she died in his arms from exposure. He got ashore at last, and had to read the burial service over his wife. He was never the same after that.

'When I knew him in the early sixties, he was a powerfully built man of the kindliest disposition. I was an invalid then, and he would sit with me for hours relating stories of his boyish scrapes or playing for hours.'

He married again, Smyth continued, and settled at Barnstaple. His wife survived for just one week after the death of her husband.

Ron Blackmore, an American whose ancestors lived in Parracombe, discovered the same story in F J Snell's 'The Blackmore Country', published in 1911.

A plaque in St Mary's Church, Molland, sheds further light on the same tale. The tablet was put up in memory of Frances Dovell, aged 47, and son William Henry, the youngest daughter and grandson of the late Henry Quartly and his wife, Elizabeth, born in Parracombe and one of the Blackmore family. They are described as the beloved wife and son of Captain William Dovell of the Port of Bristol.

The plaque describes how they perished on a voyage to the West Indies when the ship 'Adelaide' sank off the coast of Corunna in Spain. Among the 16 passengers and crew, Captain Dovell alone survived. Above the plaque is a carving of the dreadful scene.

Watts, who lived at Prisonford, also describes the funeral cortege attached to Rev Joseph Dovell, peopled by a number of clergymen.

'A hearse passed by our house with the body of the Rev Joseph Dovell followed by three mourning coaches, Rev John Pyke's carriage with three young gentlemen and three other carriages. Gentlemen present Rev J Pyke and Dr Clarke Road on horsebackbefore them the Rev J C Carwithen and Rev R J Gould, Rev R Blackmore, John Harries esq, undertaker . . . under bearers with cloaks on John Berry, J Latham, John Rook, Richard Blackmore, Thomas Lord, William Gill, C Gill – pall bearers William Crang, John Bowden, 2 Watts' and 2 Dovells (Combmartin).'

John George Berry, from Parracombe, joined the Royal Navy on 20 December 1884.

And finally, according to the 1841 census, Richard Dovell farmed at West Middleton.

(Altar tomb) 'Underneath are the remains of Elizabeth, wife of John Blackmore of this parish, who died 1 December 1859, aged 69. John, son of Richard Blackmore & Susanna, his wife, of Martinhoe, died 29 April 1778, aged 16 months. Susanna Blackmore, above, died 11 November 1778, aged 40. Richard Blackmore above, to whose memory this tomb was erected, died 28 August 1802, aged 60. William, son of William Dovell & Elizabeth his wife, grandson of Richard Blackmore, above, died 27 March 1805, aged 9 days. John Dovell, twin brother to William Dovell junior, above said, died 17 July 1824, in the 20th year of his age.

In local history notes made by Arthur Smyth in 1876, he refers to a curious superstition involving the Dovell twins that was recalled for years afterwards.

'At their birth the excise officer said that owing to a certain planet under which they were born, one would die in childhood and the other scarcely live to the age of manhood.'

On 3 September 1842 William Watts wrote: 'Put two new gravestones in Parracombe churchyard in memory of Mr Richard Blackmore, a brother of the Reverend John Blackmore, rector of Combe Martin. Also cleaned and painted his wife's gravestone. Two pounds, two shillings.'

In memory of James Dovell, died 27 October 1894, aged 83.

The only record of a James Dovell being born in Parracombe around that time is in 1817, when farmer Thomas Dovell and his wife Elizabeth, of Holworthy, had a son.

Joan Dovell, wife of William Dovell of this parish, deceased, died 12 January 1818 aged 77.

Joan and William were parents to Mary, born in 1779, and Agnes, born four years later. When she died, Joan was living in Church Town.

Elizabeth Dovell, died 20 April 1754, aged 48.

Thomas Dovell of this parish 2 July 1853, aged 81. Elizabeth his widow died 1 January 1861, aged 87.

Elizabeth Dovell b 1794

Mary b 1796

James Dovell, b 1817

Mary, daughter of William Dovell and Joan, his wife, of this parish died 5 November 1802, aged 23. Also in memory of Maria and Mary Ann (daughters of John Dovell, son of the above, William & Joan Dovell) and Mary his wife - Maria died 14 August 1802 aged 4. Mary Ann 31 October 1804, aged four months

In 1799 Joseph Dovell was born to William and Jane, who had daughter Mary in 1794.

Grace Dovell wife of Philip Dovell of this parish died 29 May 1844 in the 75th year of her age. William Dovell son of above named, died 24 November 1851, aged 49. [A William was born in 1795 but survived only weeks. A second son called William was born in 1802.]

Mary Dovell b 1799

According to William Watts, Grace Dovell's body was brought to Parracombe in a hearse from Charles.

Nathaniel Dovell died 5 October 1881 aged 85. Joanna Dovell, wife of above, died 1 April 1866 aged 57. Matilda daughter of above died 3 December 1876 aged 28.Mary Jane daughter of above died 27 October 1851 aged 20 months.

On 26 July 1846 William Watts says: 'Officiated as clerk to the church morning and afternoon when Mr Nath Dovell child called Ann was christened.' The dates imply this is the same Nathaniel.

William Dovell of this parish died 17 March 1803 aged 62. Philip Dovell son of William Dovell above & Joan, his wife, died 12 September 1809 aged 34.

Mary, daughter of William Dovell and Joan, his wife, of this parish died 5 November 1802 aged 23. Also Maria and Mary Ann, daughters of John Dovell son of above William and Joan Dovell and Mary his wife, . . (See previous inscription)

Here lies the body of Elizabeth Dovell the younger of this parish who died 28 May 1753 in the 17th year of her age.

(Altar tomb) Underneath are the remains of Jane, wife of William Dovell, gentleman of West Middleton in this parish who died 30 June 1834 in the 78th year of her age. Also the remains of the above named William Dovell who died 24 June 1835 in the 81st year of his age.

(Altar tomb) Underneath are the remains of Robert Tanner Partridge of Barnstaple who died 6 January 1888 aged 40. In memory of Sally, wife of above, who died at East Middleton 19 April 1871 aged 75. Also Richard Dovell of West Middleton who died 6 October 1872 aged 85.

Robert Tanner Partridge, from Barnstaple, married Sally Dovell in 1823.

In memory of Bartholomew Somerwill & Julia, his wife, of this Parish. Julia died Oct XV(15th), MDCCCLXVII (1867), aged LXXXIV (84) years. Bartholomew died November XXVIII (28th) MDCCCLVIII (1858), aged XC (90) years. Also two sons of the above, John Somerwill died MDCCCVII (1808) aged X (10) years and Thomas Somerwill died March XXV (25), MDCCCLV (1855), aged XXXVII (37) years.

Bartholomew, from Swimbridge, and Julia got married in 1795. In the register his surname on this occasion appears as Sammerville while her Christian name appears variously throughout as Julian to Julien. It seems John was their first son. William was born in 1804 and George in 1806. By the time Elizabeth was born in 1813 her father is described as a mason and the family are placed in Parracombe Mill. Thomas, born in 1818, seems to have been their youngest son

---

Richard Delbridge, son of John and Mary Delbridge of this parish. He died 17 May 1842, aged 18 months. The above named Mary Delbridge died 20 December 1851 aged 45.

From the dates it seems likely that John Delbridge, of 'Linton', married Mary Gammon in 1829. In 1836 they had a daughter, also called Mary, when they were living at Highley. John is described as a labourer.

William Watts describes how Mary died in the North Devon infirmary – a substantial three storey building next to Trinity Church in Barnstaple with the words 'supported by voluntary contributions emblazoned across the front - just a day after J Widdew and both were brought home in a single cart.

(This grave stone mentioned in the chapter about William Watts). To the memory of Richard Harding, son of John & Betty Harding of Trentishoe, late of this parish, died 14 August 1793, aged 8 months. Maria Harding, his sister, died at Bristol 19 April 1822, aged 25. Henry Harding, her brother, died 7 March 1834, aged 27. Rebecca Harding, his sister, died 3 October 1838, aged 26. Anna Maria Harding, daughter of William and Harriet Harding and granddaughter of John and Betty Harding before named, died 15 August 1842, aged 9. Betty Harding, above named, died 25 January 1854, aged 81. John Harding, died 26 April 1854, aged 93. Henry Harding, son of Richard and Charlotte Harding and grandson of Henry Harding, before named, died 15 February 1853, aged 1 year. Mary Slocombe, died 1 May 1844, aged 75. Henry Slocombe, died 31 May 1869, aged 79.

The Harding family was touched by tragedy and is explained more fully in the section about William Watts. But other children are thought to have survived longer, including Susannah born in 1804, Richard born in 1809 and Philip Jones, born in 1814 when this farming family's home was East Middleton.

Geneaology Notes

Charlotte, wife of John Somerwill who died 4 August 1881, aged 73.

John Sommerwill who died 2 December 1886, aged 77.

Lewis Sommerwill, son of the above, who died 17 March 1887, aged 42.

John Sommerwill, son of the above, who died 9 February 1900, aged 66.

William Sommerwill, who died 11 February 1902, aged 60

The baptism register shows John Harris Somerwell, son of mason John Somerwell and his wife Charlotte, of New House, was christened on 26 October 1834. Records indicate that John and Charlotte got married on 20th April 1833, the only wedding recorded at St Petrock's that year. Meanwhile the death of John Somerwell senior is recorded on 13 September 1807.

(Both Lewis and William are remembered but not apparently buried here.)

Elizabeth, daughter of John White, died 1 March 1889 aged 74.

Eliza, daughter of John & Mary Rook of this parish, died 14 February 1830, aged four years. Mary Rook, above named, died 26 March 1879, aged 75.

Elizabeth Rook, died 6 March 1884, aged 50. John Rook, died 19 May 1894 aged 86.

[Eliza probably not buried here as there is no entry in Parish Register.]

William Rook, son of labourer John and his wife Mary, of Heal, was baptised on 1 May 1836. The marriage of a Mary Rook and Edmund Lang is recorded on 10 November 1693. The death of a Mary Rook is recorded on 4 January 1715. It may be the birth of this Mary Rooke, recorded as the illegitimate with her mother named as Fraunces on 24 March 1620.

On 10 October 1750 a John Rooke, son of Jeffery & Dorothy Rooke, is baptised. Earlier still, a John Rooke was buried on 7 August 1598 and a John Rook was buried 16 April 1688.

Caution: This is not the Elizabeth Rook, married to Richard, who had a son, Philip, who was baptised in 1822 nor the one recorded as dying in 1751.

Roger & Sarah Hardy Buried April ye 4 1728 and November ye 27 1718.

It seems Roger and Sarah had a son, Mark, baptised on 19 January 1688.

Under this tomb are deposited the remains of Charity, wife of Richard Tucker of Martinhoe. She departed this life the 5th day of March in the year of our Lord 1798 in the 58th year of her age Epitaph. Richard Tucker above, departed this life the 2 (7?) day of June in the year of our Lord 1818 in the 78th year of his age

There is no record of Charity's burial in Parish Record.

William Blackmore of this parish, died 13 February 1891, aged 75.

William's baptism by Rev Mr Hiern is recorded on 19 February 1816, when he is recorded as the son of farmer John Blackmore and his wife Susanna, of 'Foley'. Prior to his birth the couple have twins, Richard and Susanna in 1813 and a daughter Elizabeth in 1814. Two years afterwards, when another sister, Susanna – presumably following the death of the first - arrives, the place they live is described as Voley. Christopher Blackmore arrives in 1819 and Margaret in 1822.

Records show that a William Blackmore from Parracombe joined the Royal Navy in 1827 but it's impossible to be sure it was this one, signing up as a boy.

Philip Tucker of this parish, died 5 December 1830 in the 69th year of his age. Sarah, wife of Richard Tucker of this parish, died 20 July 1859 in the 55th year of her age. William, son of above-named Philip Tucker, died 2 [9?] October 1860, aged 60. [Buried November 3 according to Parish Record]. Richard Tucker above-named, died 25 December 1860, aged 58.

This Philip Tucker is likely to be the son of Phillip and Richord Tucker, whose baptism is recorded on 10 August 1762. If so, he began life with an additional 'l' in his name. It is possible, date-wise, that he married Elizabeth Lovering in 1792 and that Philip senior died in 1816 at Bodley, aged 89. But that is guess-work. It does seem that this Philip was living at Parracombe Mill when he died.

It seems he had a brother William born in 1771, clearly not the William who is marked here. A Richard Tucker is recorded at Heale in the 1841 census.

This stone was erected by Mary Tucker to the memory of her grandfather Philip Tucker of this parish, who died 1 January 1771, aged 76. Her father Philip Tucker, died 17 December 1816, aged 89. The aforesaid Mary Tucker, died 1 May 1843, aged 86.

William Tucker junior was living at Bodley when he died. There's no trace of Mary Tucker in the records at the appropriate time. However, William Watts reports setting up a gravestone for Mary Tucker in Parracombe churchyard at a cost of one pound and ten shillings.

Richard Bowden of this parish died 2 December 1792 [buried 13 February] aged 35. Richard, his son, died 30 May 1803, aged 18. William Fulford, died 10 July 1821 aged 57. Joan, first wife to Richard Bowden above named, and second wife to William Fulford, died 29 August 1831, aged 70. Jacob Moule, of Linton (mariner) was drowned in Bude Bay 21 April 1815 aged 26. [Nothing mentioned in Parish Record.]

Richard [sic] the wife of David Berry, died 17 January 1712, in the 56th year of her age. [Yet a Richard Berry was buried 20 January 1743 according to the parish register.]

Although Richard Bowden's birth date isn't clear in the records it is apparent that he and Joan had a son, William, in 1784. Daughter Nanny had been born the previous year. A daughter, also called Joan, was born in 1788 and a son, Richard, in 1790. Thus, Joan was left with at least four small children when her husband died.

There's a marriage recorded in 1803 between William Fulford, of Buckland Brewer, and Joanna Bowden, although the exact date isn't given. The death of William Fulford, age 57, of Blue Ball Lane is recorded in 1819 while Joan is described as being from 'Linton' at the time she died. Caution: There are lots of anomalies in this!

As for David Berry, it's possible he was a noted village philanthropist, mentioned to Parliament in 1786. A return stated that one David Berry had in 1760 left £5 for the day-labourers of Parracombe, which was added to a sum of £28 left by another donor. As a result, 29 shillings was distributed by the churchwardens and overseers of the poor from parochial church funds, to poor labourers who didn't receive parochial relief.

Very much worn by weather

(Edw'd Berry] died 14 of () 1759, aged 76.

Richard Bowden of this parish died 29 December 1779, in the 61st year of his age

Richard is recorded as the son of Dauid – although this could of course be a misprint – and Dorothy Bowden, baptised on 26 December 1719

Richard Bowden of this parish died 14 September 17 [/53] in the ? Year of his age

In the records 'Richard Bowden ye younger' is recorded is being buried on 28 September 1753. Although it is impossible to say with certainty, this

may be Richard, the son of Richard and Anne Bowden, who was born in 1751.

Joanna Barwick, wife of Humphry Barwick of this parish, died 6 December 1815, aged 65. Humphry Barwick above named died 29 September 1825, aged 74.

Joanna and Humphry Barwick had son John in 1769, daughter Elizabeth the following year, son Julian in 1773, son Thomas May in 1775, son Nathaniel in 1778, son Joseph in 1780, daughter Johanna in 1785 and daughter Ann in 1788. Thomas May at least is buried at St Petrock's.

Humphry Barwick was the son of John and Elizabeth and was born in 1751. He married Johanna May in 1769. And it seems he married for a second time in 1822, to widow Mary Blackmore. When he died he was living at Parracombe Mill.

George Lovering, the elder of this parish, died June 1771 in the 82nd year of his age.

Described as 'senior' in the parish register, it seems likely he had at least one son, called George.

Richard & Eleanor Nichols of this parish he died 1792, aged 62. She died 13 January 1806 aged 8 (?4) years . Philip their son, died 20 October 1815, aged 55

Richard and Eleanor, nee Reed, married in 1753. Their first son, born in 1756, was called Phillip. But it seems the memorial in the graveyard is to a different Phillip, born in 1860 after what must have been an untimely death. There were other sons, too, Thomas (1758), Richard (1762) and William (1766).

Walter Lock, son of David Lock and Joan his wife of this parish. Died 24 February 1782, aged 11 months.

Mary Ellen, daughter of Edward and Elizabeth Cawsey, died 3 January 1897, aged 17.

John Gammin, of this parish, died 16 September 1809 in the 64th year of his age. Joan Gammin, relict of John Gammin above said, died 23 October 1849 in the 95th year of her age. Amelia Cornish, died 8 January 1896, aged 68.

With so many variations on the spelling of Gammin it's hard to know with certainty that it's the same couple but, according to the parish register, John Gamin married Joan Harding in 1776. In 1777 John and Joan Gammin had a son, John, who seems to have died three months later.

Ann, wife of Charles Nichols of this parish, died 29 June 1825 in the 36th year of her age. Charles Nichols died 26 June 1868, aged 76.

Ann and Charles, a mason of Parracombe Mill, had daughter Mary Ann in 1819. A son, James Dyer, was born in 1822.

Richard Nichols of this parish died XIV (14th) December MDCCCXXXVI (1836) in the LXXV (75) year of his age. Elizabeth, his wife, died XIII (13th) day of July AD MDCCCXLVI (1845) in her LXXXVI (84) year

Richard was born in 1762, the son of Richard and Elenor Nichols nee Reed, who married in 1753. He may have had a brother William, born in 1766 – but by this time the surname had adopted an extra letter and appeared as Nicholls. Richard Nicholls is the last person to be recorded in the register we are using. He died at Parracombe Mill.

Robert Thomas, elder of this parish, died 25 March 1766, aged 87 years

---

Robert Thomas, of this parish of Kentisbury, died 20 July 1790 in the 82nd year of his age.

It seems likely this Robert Thomas was born to Robert and Mary Thomas nee Gammon in 1708, earlier described as 'a tayler'.

Agnes Berry, daughter of John & Emme Berry of this parish, died 15 April 1833 in the 11th year of her age. 'A pious youth lies sleeping here, beloved of parents and sister dear'.

Agnes is recorded as living in Bumsley and her parents were John, a farmer, and Emma. She had at least one sister, Ann, born in 1817.

George Gibbs of this parish, died 17 September 1862 in the 81st year of his age. Betty Gibbs, wife of above named, died 17 February 1875 aged 89. 'Farewell my children dear'.

George and Betty had a son, John, in 1821 when they were living at Little Rowley when George was described as a farmer. Two years later, a daughter, Mary, is recorded to George Gibbs at Little Rowley but this time he is called a labourer and the mother's full name is given as Elizabeth.

By 1828 when another son, James, is born George is once again called a farmer and the mother is Elizabeth. The marriage of George, of Loxhore, and Elizabeth Fry is recorded in 1808.

Sarah, wife of Joseph Hill of this parish died 8 December 1884 aged 68. The above named Joseph Hill, died 30 October 1885, aged 62.

Philip Geen, buried 9 March 1741, aged 31.

The circumstances of the Geen family are cloaked in mystery. Logic puts the birth of this Phillip in 1709, where he is recorded as the son of Phillip and Trephoena. In 1722 a son, Alexander, is born to a Phillip and Typhony Geen, presumably a brother to the above. The wedding of Phillip Nicholls, with the alias of Geen, to Elizabeth Lusimore, took place in 1733. In the same year a son, Phillip, is recorded to Richard and Elizabeth Geen, alias Nicholls. Could this been an error by the recorder, switching the son and husband's names? Daughters Mary and Grace arrived in 1734 and 1736 respectively, both with the alias Nicholls.

Mary Barwick, wife of Richard Barwick of this parish, d 11 May 1861, aged 76. Richard Barwick, died 1 April 1865, aged 83. Nathaniel, son of above, died 17 December 1883, aged 56.

In 1827 Mary and her labourer husband Richard, of Holwell, had twin sons, Joseph and Nathaniel.

Elizabeth Gill, daughter of Thomas and Mary Gill of this parish, died 14 April 1822, aged 3. Thomas Gill, above, died 25 December 1848, aged 72. 'Farewell dear wife, children, friends . . . ' Mary Gill, died 26 December 1878, aged 94.

It seems likely that Elizabeth had a brother, William, born in 1807 but there's no certainty about her birth according to the records, although an Elizabeth Gale is noted in 1819 to a Thomas and Mary Gale, of Little Bumsley. No date is given for the baptism. The death of three year old Elizabeth Gale of Little Bumsley is recorded in April 1823.

There's more certainty about the headstone, thanks to William Watts' diary. It was put up in August 1849 at a cost of one pound nineteen shillings and sixpence.

George Tucker, son of Philip Tucker deceased and Elizabeth his wife of this parish, died 6 May 1838 in the 32nd year of his age. Agnes Tucker, daughter of Philip and Elizabeth Tucker, above named, died 6 June 1844 in the 36th year of her age.

The birth of George Tucker is recorded in September 1806, the son of Philip and Elizabeth Tucker.

William Watts charged 12 shillings and six pence to set up Agnes Tucker's gravestone.

William Burgess, of this parish, died 2 June 1743 (?), aged 31

Epitaph only: 'Farewell my loving wife and children . . . '

It's impossible to know if this is the same William Burgess who married Elizabeth Babb in 1741.

Robert Moon, of this parish, died 11 April 1809 in the 74th year of his age. Thomasin, wife of Robert Moon, above, died 22 April 1827 in the 82nd year of her age.

Robert and Thomasin are recorded as having six children; Robert born in 1767, Thomas in 1771, Richard in 1775, Elizabeth in 1777, Thomasin in 1782 and Mary in 1793. Mum Thomasin - whose name appears as Thomasine and also Thomazine, lived at Bodley when she died. Her daughter Thomasin married John Davells of Barnstaple in 1811.

(Altar tomb) Mary Lock, daughter of John and Charity Lock of this parish, died 14 June 1848, aged 72. Richard Lovering senior of this parish (and for whom this tomb was erected), died 28 March 1849 aged 71 years. Elizabeth Lovering, relict of Richard Lovering beforenamed, died 1 February 1850, aged 70. Elizabeth Lock Roach, daughter of above named Richard Lovering, died at Akron, State of New York, 22 October 1856, aged 35. John, son of above Richard and Elizabeth Lovering and husband of Elizabeth Lovering of this parish, d 18 January 1858, aged 47. All the above are interred under this slab, except E L Roach who died at Akron 1856.

Richard Lovering was born in 1778, the son of George and Mary Lovering. In 1808, he married Elizabeth Lock and six children are subsequently recorded. Mary Ann was born in 1809, John arrived the following year and, when Eleanor was born in 1814, Richard is described as a blacksmith at 'Paracomb Mill'. His details remain the same when Richard arrived in 1816 and William, two years after that. But when Elizabeth Lock Lovering was born in 1821, her father is described as a maltster.

John Smyth, died 20 March 1897, aged 88.

Born in 1807 at nearby Charles, North Devon, John was married to Richord Tucker – remembered on the memorial below - and farmed 100 acres around East Hill.

Elizabeth Tucker, relict of Philip Tucker of this parish, died 27 June 1846, in the 78th year of her age. Mary Tucker, daughter of the above, died 26 October 1879, aged 74. Richord, w of John Smyth of East Hill and daughter of the above and Philip Tucker, died 3 January 1880, aged. 69. Elizabeth Comer, sister of above, died 6 November 1882 aged 84. Henry Comer, husband of above, died 24 March 1908 aged 98.

Elizabeth Tucker was born in 1836 to farmer John and wife Richord Smyth, of Parracombe Mill. Henry has been born at Skillaton where his father John, a labourer, and mother Winifred lived. Although his age is recorded as 98, his baptism record says he was born in 1816, making him 94.

To memory of Charlotte Allison, wife of Robert St John Allison, died at Parracombe 6 October 1897 aged 71.

Here lies Henry Harding the elder of this parish who died 18 January 1781, aged 87. In memory of Mary Harding, relict of John Harding of this parish, who died 3 May 1823 in the 93rd year of her age, also Grace Harding, daughter of John & Mary Harding above named, who died 27 December 1854 in the ---- year of her age (broken off).

In the parish record of his death, Henry Harding seems to be recorded as Herding.

Here lies Joan, wife of Henry Harding of this parish of 9th (November?) 17 - - in the 3 - - year of her age. Mary, daughter of Henry Harding of this parish, died 24 July 1751.

Joan's name is also recorded as Herding at her death, on 28 March 1780, as is Mary's. Mary lived at East Middleton.

Nicholas Ridd of this parish, died 15 February 1815, aged 76.

There's no apparent record of Nicholas' death in 1815 although Mary Ridd, of East Hill, died in February that year aged 76.

William, son of William and Mary Harton, of this parish, died 26 May 1847, aged 14. William Harton, last named, died 14 January 1862, aged 71. Mary Harton, died 2 March 1877, aged 75. M A Way, died 8 December 1880, aged 52. Ellen Harton, died 12 April 1889, aged 50, interred at Ilfracombe. Ann Richards, died 4 October 1890, aged 64, interred at Calverleigh

---

(Altar tomb) Eleanor Roach, wife of Richard Roach of this parish, died 16 October 1782, aged 63. 'Lamented by children dear . . . ' Richard Roach, above said, died 24 February 1785, aged 76. Mary, daughter of Richard Roach and Joan, his wife, died 30 January 1791, aged 7 days. Charles, their son, died 16 May 1799 in the second year of his age.

Eleanor is recorded as Helena and her death noted as 1781 in the parish record. Her son, also called Richard, was born in 1757. Another son, William, was born in 1760 while in 1764 Joseph came along. It seems likely that Eleanor - recorded again as Helena - Harton married Richard Roach in 1750.

William Hoyles, husband of Agnes Hoyles, died 2 March 1898, aged 78.

Agness Lancey, wife of John Lancey of this parish, died 20 May 1838 aged 76. John Lancey, above, died 17 August 1818, aged 81.

Alternatively spelled Agnes Lancy, she was the mother of Mary, born in 1790, John, born in 1792, Richard, 1795, Thomas, 1798, James born in 1802 and Rebecca in 1804.

When they married in 1790, John Lancy was listed as a shoemaker. Agnes' maiden name was Smyth. Neither were found in the death records.

Susanna, wife of John Blackmore of this parish, died 27 February 1807, aged 37. Also John [rest buried]

Susanna and John had sons John in 1796, William in 1800, twins Richard and Susanna in 1813 when as farmers they lived at 'Foley', Elizabeth in 1814, William in 1816 and another Susanna in 1818. John died in 1835.

Thomas, son of John and Agnes Gibbs of this parish, died 8 October 1873, aged 6.

Agnes Gibbs [sic] died 22 November 1906, aged 82. John Gibbs, husband of the above, died 15 December 1906, aged 85.

It seems likely that this John Gibbs was born to farmer George Gibbs and his wife Betty, of Little Rowley in 1821. He had a brother, James, born in 1828.

Fred Gibbs, died 23 June 1903, aged 34.

James Gibbs, died 18 August 1913, aged 60.

John Blackmore of this parish, died 31 August 1835, in 73rd year of his age. Agnes, wife of William Blackmore, died 31 August 1857, aged 55. William Blackmore, above named, died 13 March 1880, aged 79. Hannah, wife of the above William Blackmore, died 11 February 1902, aged 82.

In the parish records John Blackmore is said to be

71 and living at Parracombe Lane at the time of his death on 3 September 1835. His first wife Susanna is remembered in the graveyard.

(Altar Tomb) Here lyeth Mary, daughter of John Lock of this parish and Joane, his wife, buried 28 September 1716, in the 23rd year of her age. 'A virgin fair was buried here . . . ' By the S side of this to be lies the body of Alice Crang of this parish, widow, who died 6 April 1763 in the 77th year of her age. Also here lies the body of Agnes, daughter of above John Lock, died 19 June 1767, aged 76.

In the register Mary's mother is named as Johan and the surname is spelled Locke.

It seems likely that Alice was married to Richard Crang and was the mother of Mary, born in 1717 and Elizabeth, born in 1724.

Near this stone lie the bodies of two sons and one daughter of Richard Crang and Joane, his wife, originally of this parish. Mary, died 7 October 1749, in the 6th year of her age. William, died 16 May 1749 in his infancy, Richard, died 6 September - - -

---

Walter Crang of Martinhoe, died 1 January 1813, in the 37th year of his age.

(Altar tomb) Here resteth Francis Lock, of Crosscombe, in the parish of Martinhoe, died 12 January 1741, aged 81. 'My loving wife and children sweet . . . ' Also here lies the body of Mary, wife of Francis Lock abovnamed, who died 2 December 1772, in the 87th year of her age. Also here under this tomb lye th the body of John Lock, father of Francis Lock, died 4 June 1712, aged 41.

Sally Cooke, died at Parracombe Mills 7 July 1876, aged 81.

(Altar tomb) Underneath are the remains of Samuel, son of Charles and Eleanor Blackmore of this parish who died 24 November 1846, aged 18 days. Francis Lock, son of above names died 22 November 1851, aged 16 months. Samuel Lovering, son of above said died 23 January 1855, aged two months. Elizabeth Blackmore, daughter of above, died 16 December 1863, aged 18. Mary Ann Lock Blackmore, another daughter, died 10 January 1864, aged 16. Josiah Blackmore, only surviving son of above said Charles and Eleanor Blackmore, died 21 August 1876, aged 20. Emma, wife of William Southall and third daughter of the above named Charles and Eleanor Blackmore, who died 1 June 1882, aged 30. The above named Eleanor Blackmore, died 15 September 1884, aged 70. The above names Charles Blackmore, died 25 May 1894, aged 84. On S side, William Lock, son of Walter Lock and Margaret, his wife, of this parish, buried 28 November 1759, aged two months. Mary, their daughter, buried on the s side of this grave, 17 June 1762, in the second year of her age. On E said only, Epitaph only. On N side Here lies the body of David, son of David Lock of this parish, who died 4 June 1742, aged 6 months. Also, here lies the body of William, son of Walter Lock of this parish, died 24 November 1759, aged 9 weeks. On W side, David Lock of this parish died 28 January 1815, in the 72nd year of his age.

Here lies the body of John Crang of Kentisbury, died 21 August 1778 in the 65th year of his age.

(Altar tomb) John Crang senior, of this parish, died 28 December 1798, aged 54. Elizabeth Crang, wife of above mentioned John Crang, died 13 May 1819, aged 82. 'A loving wife and tender parent'.

There are many John Crangs in the records with John Crang 'ye younger' dying in 1762 and John Crang 'ye youngest' dying in 1748. A line of John Crangs lived at Walner. When she died, Elizabeth Crang was recorded as living at Becot in Arlington. She may well have been the mother of Betty, born in 1770, Richard, born in 1774 and Walter, 1776.

(Altar tomb) On top Underneath are the remains of John Crang of this parish, died 27 February 1835, in the 64th year of his age. Also of Jane Charley, wife of John Charley and daughter of John Crang, above named and Dorcas his wife, died 4 July 1838 in the 28th year of her age. Also of Richard Crang son of above, died 9 April 1839 in the 34th year of his age. John Crang, son of John and Mary Crang of Walnor of this parish & grandson of the above John and Dorcas Crang, died at Hong Kong, 7 December 1856, aged 18. Also of Dorcas, wife of John Crang, above mentioned, died 1 July 1859, aged 90. Also of John Crang, son of John and Dorcas Crang above named, died 15 November 1860, aged 60. Also of Elizabeth, daughter of John and Mary Crang, above named, died 3 May 1864, aged 16. Richard Crang on of above, died 28 March 1866, aged 22.

Grace Slader, daughter of John Slader deceased and Joan his wife of this parish, died 2 June 1803 in the 22nd year of her age.

Grace was born to John Slader senior and Joan in 1781.

Nicholas Blackmore, son of Nicholas Blackmore and Mary his wife of this parish died 24 May 1807 in the 22nd year of his age. Nicholas Blackmore, son of above name, died 28 June 1818, aged 66.

According to records, Nicholas Blackmore, 'a taylor', married Mary Knight in June 1776. They had a daughter, Mary, in 1776. Three years later, there came another daughter, Rebecca and in 1782, a third, Nancy – who married sailor Thomas Fry in 1805. Nicholas was born in 1785 followed by Richard in 1789. The records show that Nicholas Blackmore drowned at Heddon's Mouth with John Lane. When Nicholas senior died he was living at Parracombe Mill.

Rebecca Smith wife of Thomas Smith of this parish, died 1 February 1857 aged 78.

Rebecca Blackmore had married Thomas Smith in 1824.

John Lancey of this parish d 22 April 1855 aged 62. Elizabeth wife of above, died 17 March 1879 aged 87.

It seems John Lancey married Elizabeth Blackmore in 1814.

Mary Grace, daughter of Richard and Mary Bowden of this parish, died 19 September 1867 aged five weeks. John, infant son of above named, died 25 February 1870. Alice Anne, daughter of the above named died 11 May 1870 aged four years.

Another tale of untimely deaths among children, this time affecting the Bowden family. But none of the above are mentioned in these parish records.

Mary, wife of Richard Bowden of this parish, died 20 October 1899, aged 59.

William Spurrier, died 27 July 1883, aged 77. Jane Spurrier, wife of above, 11 April 1888 aged 75.

John Tossell died 26 December 1873 aged 75. Ann, wife of above named, died 2 April 1878 aged 76.

Labourer John married Ann Spuryer (a name that morphed into both Spuryar and Spurrier) in 1824 and they lived at Tucking Mill. Their first child, Mary, was baptised on their wedding anniversary a year later. Five other children – Thomas, William, Maria, John and James - followed at two year intervals.

Here lies the body of Thomas Roach of this parish died 19 June 17 (?34). Also here lieth the body of Isot (?) Roach, wife of Thomas Roach died 12 December 1754 in the 54th year of her age.

According to birth records, daughter Elizabeth was born to Isaat, nee Tooker, in November 1734, five months after Thomas' death. The couple had married early the same year.

Lieutenant John Whitefield RN, died 22 January 1821 aged 35. Eliza Whitefield, daughter of James & Ann Whitefield of this parish (who erected this stone) died 30 October 1834 aged 5 1/2. Her sister Mary Ann Whitefield died 5 December 1835, aged 4 1/2. Eliza Ann, another daughter of above died 24 December 1857 in the 22nd year of her age. James Whitefield died 23 July 1868 aged 72. Ann Whitefield 15 April 1882, aged 86.

James Whitefield was a tailor who lived with wife Ann at Parracombe Mill. It must be presumed that Lt Whitefield was his brother as a son, John, wasn't born until 1827. Eliza was born in 1829, Mary Ann in 1831 and Eliza Ann in 1836. There's no further record of children born to James and Ann.

Mary, wife of the late John Haskings died 5 April 1865 aged 65.

John, from Charles, and Mary married in 1837.

Richard Crocombe, Bon 20 March 1820 died 1 January 1889. Sarah Crocombe his wife born 14 July 1833, died 16 August 1900.

(Altar tomb) On top Underneath are the remains of Grace Parminster Lock, wife of William Lock of this parish, she died 4 May 1851 aged 70 years. Also the remains of above named William Lock who died 23 July 1860 aged 77. Also William Lock of East Bodley who died 2 February 1886 aged 66. Also of Elizabeth Lock, widow of the above who died at Barnstaple 20 January 1909 aged 80. Also of Emily Ann Lock, daughter of the above who died at Barnstaple 17 August 1897 aged 32.

Grace's full name appears only twice in the records, at the birth of daughter Mary Ann in 1814 and son John two years later. But as Grace, she appears in 1819, as mother to William and 1824 as the mother of Thomas. She and her farmer husband lived at Bodley. William Lock was born in 1782, the son of John and Charity Lock who were themselves married in 1775.

From William Watts' diary it appears Grace's gravestone cost 17 shillings and sixpence – or perhaps that was the price of engraving.

Mary Smyth, wife of James H Smyth of Bodley died 25 November 1870 aged 66. Also to the memory of James H Smyth above died named who died 2 June 1883 aged 67. Also Frederick George, son of Henry & Betsy Smyth, died 26 January 1866 aged 1 year. Also Maria, daughter of the above who died 23 February 1889 aged 3 days. Also Betsy, wife of Henry Smyth died 29 June 1889 aged 33. Also Meta Ann, daughter of the above died 6 April 1909 aged 26. Also Charity wife of the above died 18 March 1912 aged 63.

Elizabeth Smyth, daughter of James Huxtable Smyth & Mary his wife of this parish died 28 December 1816 (?) aged nine months.

James Huxtable Smyth was the brother of George, the builder of the Wesleyan Chapel , himself born in North Molton while wife Mary came from Martinhoe. Henry, one of their seven children, was buried his first wife, Betsy, four months after their baby daughter Maria died. His second wife was Charity, one of many burials that took place after the opening of Christ Church.

To further muddy the waters, Williams Watts records putting up a headstone, at a cost of one pound two shillings and 6 pence to an unnamed child of Mary and William. He describes the monument as 'a neat one'.

Grace, wife of Thomas Tossell died 22 November 1893 aged 58. Sarah Tossell, daughter of above died 29 October 1890 aged 21. Thomas Tossell, husband of above, died 14 January 1903 aged 76.

Agnes Pearce of this parish wife of Zachariah Pearce, native of Wiveliscombe, Somerset, died 18 April 1852, aged 46. Zachariah Pearce, died 22 April 1892 aged 77. Also Sarah Pearce, who died 27 October 1908 aged 64.

Joan, wife of Jonathan Seldon, died 1 February 1862, aged 51. Jonathan Seldon, died 23 April 1870 aged 66.

Joan and Jonathan – a labourer living at Rowley - had a daughter, Mary Ann, in 1833 a year after the couple were married.

Mary Ann Tossell wife of James Tossell, died 2 July 1911 aged 78. Bessie, daughter of above died 1864 aged 7 months.

James Tossell was born to parents John and Ann, of Tucking Mill in 1835. At the turn of the century, a Mrs Tossell was running a laundry and the vicinity of today's village hall was known as 'the drying field'.

Emma Berry, died 6 February 1868, aged 21. William Berry died 13 February 1888, aged 75. Sarah Berry, wife of above died 24 October 1895, aged 80.

William Gill of this parish died 9 March 1887 aged 80.

The son of Thomas and Mary Gill, William was born in 1807.

William Rottenbury died 30 April 1863 aged 29. Humphrey Rottenbury died at Lynton 6 June 1878 aged 71. Mary, his wife, died at Parracombe 2 November 1888 aged 82.

William, only son of George and Eliza Linscott died 25 October 1874 aged 4 years. George Linscott died 29 December 1875, aged 42.

John Bray of this parish died 26 November 1887 aged 68. Jane Bray wife of above died 12 March 1910 aged 78.

William Bourn June died 1 February 1883 aged 32. William Bourn, father of above, died 12 January 1901 aged 81.

John Crocombe, late of Holworthy died 15 August 1881 aged 63. Grace, wife of above, died 11 July 1901 aged 91. Mary Crocombe, daughter of above died 13 November 1910 aged 64.

James Carr of this parish died 12 December 1882 aged 84. Grace, wife of above, died 1 January 1876, aged 82. Herbert Tom Carr, grandson of above, died 2 April 1874 aged 4 months. Mary Carr, daughter of above, died 11 May 1893 aged 63.

James Carr was born in 1797 or 1798 to Thomas and Margery Carr. It seems like his marriage to Grace took place elsewhere but children Susan, Mary, Eliza, Betsy and finally Charles were recorded in Parracombe after being born at Heale.

Jane, eldest daughter of John & Mary Crang died at Walmer 18 August 1870 aged 30.

Martha Polkinghorne daughter of Alfred and Sarah Polkinghorne died 12 February 1850 aged 8 years.

At the time, Alfred Polkinghorne was the licensee of the London Inn and was also the village baker.

Eleanor Smyth b 18 March 1814, died 17 February 1887.

Elizabeth Smyth born 2 July 1822, died 19 September 1888.

Eleanor and Elizabeth were both spinster sisters of George and James Huxtable Smyth.

Harold Percy, son of Arthur and Bessie Smyth, born 6 March 1887, died 30 June 1889.

Richard Harton of this parish died 9 July 1817, aged 72. Elizabeth Harton, relict of Richard Harton above, she died 19 December 1845, aged 85.

Richard Harton was born in 1745 to parents Richard and Joan Harton. He became a father at 49 when his son, also called Richard, was born in 1794. A daughter, Eleanor, died in 1772. When Richard senior died he was living at Parracombe Mill. It's presumably Richard Harton junior who is recorded in the 1841 census at 'Parracombe Mill Village'.

John Lean of the parish of Swimbridge, who died 24 May 1807, aged 32.

Here lyeth body of Richard Tucker, died 1st April 1728. Also here lyeth body of Elizabeth Tucker his wife who died 20 April 1743 aged 73. Here lies the body of Mary, wife of John Geen who died 3 July 1763 aged 55.

As if by way of a joke on the genealogists that followed, Richard Tucker - who was buried on 1 April - appears as Tooker in the records. It's only guesswork that says it is this Richard Tucker who married Ellizabeth Moon in 1715.

Mary Gammon, daughter of Joseph Gammon, deceased, and Mary his wife, originally of this parish. She was buried in her father's grave 7 March 1803 aged 16. [Both these names have been changed from Gammin to Gammon.]

Joseph Gammon, son of Joseph Gammon and Mary his wife originally of this parish. He died 19 March 1801 aged 20.

There's evidence that Joseph and Mary, who were married by the Curate of Challacombe in 1773, had at least one other child, John, born in 1774.

Here lies the body of Elizabeth, the daughter of Thomas Nichols of this parish who died 19 February 1765 in the 34th year of her age.

Here lies the body of Margaret Gammon, relict of John Gammon of this parish. She died 12 November 1798.

Records reveal that Margaret gave birth to nine children in 18 years. To give insight on the scale of her loss, three were called John and two were named Mary, indicating she lost at least a third of her off-spring.

Here lieth the body of Richard Harton of this parish who was buried 15 June 172- - (1724, according to parish record)

Here lyeth the body of Joan, wife of Henry Harding of this parish, died 28 November 1746, aged 46.

Here lies the body of William Thomas of the parish of Kentisbury, died 17 September 1758, aged 54.

Here lies the body of William Thomas of this parish, died 1 August 1786 in the 39th year of his age.

Here lies the body of Walter, son of David Lock and Joan his wife of this parish who died 2 December 1782 aged 21 weeks.

Mary Lancey, daughter of John Lancey and Joan, his wife, of this parish, died 24 February 1810 aged 27.

Here lies the body of Samuel Litson, son of Richard Litson & Mary, his wife, of Linton. He died 2nd April 1785 in the 39th year of his age.

Exmoor Girl

Inspired by a grave in St Petrock's churchyard

Up here the long grass clothed us all,
Old trees lent on the churchyard wall,
A buzzard spiked his piercing call.

Inside the church the words stood clear –
There is no man that we should fear,
But only God, forever near.

On Sundays, in our sombre hue,
The family would take our pew,
We knew our place, as we should do.

We kept our fields, one milching cow,
White geese, a Gloucester Black-Spot sow.
All that is distant from me now.

Our world was small, this sunlit combe
Welcomed our heaving from the womb,
Gave up her earth to bed our tomb.

Down this short path they carried me,
'Oh Lord, wee'm brung a gift to 'ee,
'Old in they 'eart, young Charity.'

In faith and hope my years were spent,
Touch, sight and smell were only leant.
I held them once – I am content.

Avril Newey

Bibliography and references

Addleshaw, G.W.O. and Etchells, F. 1948 The Architectural Setting of Anglican Worship, London: Faber and Faber.

Ashworth, E. 1881 'Notes on some North Devon Churches', Transactions of the Exeter Diocesan Architectural Society Second Series 5, 6–15.

Ashworth, Edward c.1866 West Country Churches: Notes and Sketches, 2 volumes: DHC Z19/18/2 a–b.

Ashworth, Edward 1915 'Notes of West Country churches: Cornwall, Devon, Somerset', bound typescript in West Country Studies Library [ref: s726.5/WES/ASH].

Ashworth, Edward various dates Seven sketchbooks in the D&EI [ref: SW cupboard 1896 ASH X].

Anon. n.d. 'Illustrated Manuscript of historical and architectural information on the churches in the Deanery of Shirwell in the Archdeaconry of Barnstaple. This impressive document comprises 2-7 pages on each of the following churches: Ashford, Berrynarbor, Bittadon, Braunton, Brendon, Challacombe, Charles, Combmartin, Countisbury, Georgeham, Goodleigh, Heanton, Highbray, Ilfracombe, Kentisbury, Lee Chapel, Loxhore, Lynton, Martinhoe, Marwood, Morthoe, Parracombe, Shirwell, Stoke Rivers, Trentishoe, West Buckland, West Down. Written in a small neat hand with drawings and watercolours of architectural details in the text and tipped in, some full page. Including drawings of features such as stained glass windows, recumbent monument figures, carved communion table rails, carved ceilings, columns, rubbings of brass inscriptions, reredos, fonts, floor plans, views of the exterior, coats of arms, etc. Purchased by FoDA and deposited in Devon Heritage Centre (DHC ref: 8757Z/1: 'North Devon Churches').'

Blackmore, David R. 2001 Parracombe: Arthur Smyth's history of Parracombe 1876, Chester: Blackmore Books.

Blaylock, S.R. and Bishop, P.J.F. 1993 St Mary's Church, Bratton Clovelly, Devon: Recording of Wall Paintings, 1993, Exeter Museums Archaeological Field Unit Report 93.31. [DHC 8264A/1/93.31]

Bulmer-Thomas, Ivor n.d. Guide to St Petrock's, Parracombe, London: Redundant Churches Fund.

Bulmer-Thomas, Ivor 1987 Guide to St Petrock's, Parracombe (revised 1987), London: Redundant Churches Fund.

Bulmer-Thomas, Ivor 2006 Church of St Petrock, Parracombe, Devon, London: Churches Conservation Trust, text as Bulmer Thomas 1987, with new illustrations by Christopher Dalton.

Chatfield, M. 1989 Churches the Victorians Forgot, Ashbourne: Moorland Publishing.

Cherry, B. and Pevsner, N. 1989 The Buildings of England: Devon. Revised ed'n, London: Penguin Books.

Clarke, Basil, F.L. 1963 The Building of the

Eighteenth-Century Church, London: SPCK.

Cresswell, B.F. 1924 Notes on Devon Churches: The Fabric and Features of Interest in the Churches of the Deanery of Shirwell, typescript volume in Westcountry Studies Library, Exeter.

Davidson, James n.d. [1830s-40s] 'Church Notes, North of Devon' bound ms. in Westcountry Studies Library, Exeter [WSL W 726.5/DEV/DAV; now DHC G2/12/6/1].

Davies, Kathryn 2008 Artisan Art: Vernacular wall paintings in the Welsh Marches, 1550–1650, Hereford: Logaston Press.

EDAS 1845–¬66 'Rough Notes for correction on the Churches of Devon and Cornwall collected by the Exeter Diocesan Architectural Society in 1845–1866', 29 printed folio sheets, Exeter: The Society.

Gray, Todd 2011 Devon's Fifty Best Churches, Exeter: The Mint Press.

Farrington, Karen 2004 Parracombe and the Heddon Valley: an unfinished history, Parracombe: Parracombe Archaeology and History Society.

Fernie, E. 2000 The Architecture of Norman England, Oxford: O.U.P.

Fernie, Eric 2014 Romanesque Architecture, The First Style of the European Age, (The Pelican History of Art), New Haven and London: Yale University Press.

Hamling, Tara 2010 Decorating the 'Godly' Household: religious Art in Post-Reformation Britain, New Haven and London: Yale University Press.

Latham, H.R. 1994 'The Parracombe scrap-book of H.R. Latham: newspaper cuttings' notes from 1890's to recent times. Photocopy donation to NDRO. [Parracombe]: Publisher W. Delbridge; North Devon Record Office BN:PAR7/0001/PAR].

McDermott, M. and Berry, S. (eds) 2011 Edmund Rack's Survey of Somerset, Taunton: Somerset Archaeological and Natural History Society.

Newman, J. and Pevsner, N. 2006 The Buildings of England: Shropshire (new edition), New Haven and London: Yale University Press.

Orbach, J. and Pevsner, N. 2014 The Buildings of England, Somerset: South and West, New Haven and London: Yale University Press.

Scott, J., Mack, F. and Clarke, J. 2007a Towers & Bells of Devon, Part 1: History of Towers, Bells, Bell-Foundries, Bell Hangers & Ringers, 1 of 2 vols, Exeter: The Mint Press.

Scott, J., Mack, F. and Clarke, J. 2007b Towers & Bells of Devon, Part 2: Abbot's Bickington to Zeal Monachorum, 2 of 2 vols, Exeter: The Mint Press.

Skinner, A.J.P. and Chanter, J.F. 1917 The Register of Baptisms, Marriages & Burials of the Parish of Parracombe, Devon 1597–1836, Exeter: The Devon & Cornwall Record Society.

Smyth, Arthur 1930[?] The History of Parracombe, unpublished typescript in North Devon Athenaeum [ref: DMSS/900/PAR].

Stabb, J. 1908 Some Old Devon Churches: Their Rood Screens, Pulpits, Fonts, etc., London: Simpkin, Marshall, Hamilton, Kent & Co.

Stabb, J. 1909 Devon Church Antiquities: Being a Description of Many Objects of Interest in the Old Parish Churches of Devonshire, London: Simpkin, Marshall, Hamilton, Kent & Co.

Stabb, J. 1911 Some Old Devon Churches: Their Rood Screens, Pulpits, Fonts, etc: Volume II, London: Simpkin, Marshall, Hamilton, Kent & Co.

Stabb, J. 1916 Some Old Devon Churches: Their Rood Screens, Pulpits, Fonts, etc: Volume III, London: Simpkin, Marshall, Hamilton, Kent & Co .

Webster, Thomas (1800–1886) A Village Choir

(1847), oil on canvas © Victoria & Albert Museum (FA 222[O]).

William Watt's Diary (unpublished)

Interview with Gilbert Walters, 2003

Blackmores of Parracombe: The Migrants to USA by David Blackmore

Blackmores of Parracombe: Some Black Sheep? By David Blackmore

Parracombe: Henry Blackmore's Memoir by David Blackmore

Blackmores of Parracombe: Letters of Reuben Blackmore by David Blackmore

National Archives

North Devon Records Office

Dwelly's Parish Records

Devon & Cornwall Record Society 1917

Arthur Smyth's 'History of Parracombe'

Acknowledgements

I am very grateful to Thomas Thurlow of Exmoor National Park, for commissioning the lecture on which they are based; to my co-presenter Meriel O'Dowd of the Churches Conservation Trust; and to Linda Blanchard and Karen Farrington of the Parracombe Archaeology and History Society for prompting me to get my thoughts on paper. Also to Simon Cartlidge, Hugh Harrison and Pru Manning for helpful discussion of aspects of the church and its furnishings.

Stuart Blaylock

Printed in Great Britain
by Amazon